The New Americans
Recent Immigration and American Society

Edited by
Steven J. Gold and Rubén G. Rumbaut

A Series from LFB Scholarly

The Outsider Entrepreneurs

R. Isil Yavuz

LFB Scholarly Publishing LLC
El Paso 2014

Copyright © 2014 by LFB Scholarly Publishing LLC

All rights reserved.

Library of Congress Cataloging-in-Publication Data

Yavuz, R. Isil, 1979-
  The outsider entrepreneurs / R. Isil Yavuz.
      pages cm -- (The new Americans: recent Immigration and American society)
  Includes bibliographical references and index.
  ISBN 978-1-59332-715-6 (hardcover : alk. paper)
  1. Businesspeople. 2. Immigrants. 3. Entrepreneurship. 4. Business enterprises, Foreign. 5. New business enterprises. 6. High technology industries--Social aspects--United States. I. Title.
  HB615.Y396 2013
  338'.040869120973--dc23
                                                     2013029600

ISBN 978-1-59332-715-6

Printed on acid-free 250-year-life paper.

Manufactured in the United States of America.

Table of Contents

List of Tables vii

List of Figures ix

Preface xi

Acknowledgements xiii

CHAPTER 1 An Introduction: Outsider Entrepreneurs, Firm Strategy and Performance 1

CHAPTER 2 Early Internationalization as a Firm Strategy 7

CHAPTER 3 Immigrant Entrepreneurship (IE) and a Conceptual Clarification: Outsider versus Insider Entrepreneurs 21

CHAPTER 4 Early Internationalization and Performance: Does Outsiderness Matter? 29

CHAPTER 5 The Context of the Study 41

CHAPTER 6 Outsider Entrepreneurs: More International but not More Successful 53

CHAPTER 7 Field Interviews 83

CHAPTER 8 Discussion of Findings 103

CHAPTER 9 Conclusion: Contributions, Limitations and Future Research Directions 117

Appendix A 127

Appendix B 129
Appendix C 133
Appendix D 137
Appendix E 139
References 143
Index 159

List of Tables

Table 1: Number of firms in 2007 (year 3) 44
Table 2: Variable Definitions 47
Table 3: Descriptive Statistics 54
Table 4: Pairwise Correlations 55
Table 5: Comparison of the Means of Key Variables for Immigrant vs. Native-Founded New Ventures 56
Table 6: Comparison of the Means of Key Variables for Domestic-Only vs. International New Ventures 57
Table 7: Test of H1: Logistic Estimate of the Likelihood of Early Internationalization 59
Table 8: Test of H2a: Instrumental Variable Probit (ivprobit) Estimation of Firm Survival 61
Table 9: Test of H2b: Instrumental Variable Regression (ivreg) Estimation Effect of Firm Growth 62
Table 10: Test of H3a: Probit Estimate of Firm Survival 65
Table 11: Test of the Interaction Effect between Early Internationalization and Immigrant Status on Firm Growth 69
Table 12: Test of H3b: Ordinary Least Square (OLS) Estimate of Firm Growth 72
Table 13: Summary Analysis of Results 77

Table 14: Robustness Test: Ordered Probit Estimate of
International Sales Intensity (% of Foreign Sales)............... 79

Table 15: Robustness Test. The Probit Estimate of Early
Internationalization with Different Measures of
Outsiderness.. 80

Table 16: Description of the Cases 84

Table 17: Profile of Outsider versus Insider Entrepreneurs and
their New Ventures 87

Table 18: Comparison of the Means of Key Variables for
Immigrant vs. Native-Founded International New
Ventures... 115

List of Figures

Figure 1: Theoretical Model 40

Figure 2: Total number of high-tech firms in the sample 43

Figure 3: Moderating Effect of Early Internationalization Strategy on the Relationship between Founders' Immigrant Status and Firm Survival 66

Figure 4: Moderating Effect of Founders' Immigrant Status on the Relationship between Early Internationalization Strategy and Firm Survival 68

Figure 5: Moderating Effect of Early Internationalization Strategy on the Relationship between Founders' Immigrant Status and Firm Growth 73

Figure 6: Moderating Effect of Founders' Immigrant Status on the Relationship between Early Internationalization Strategy and Firm Growth 74

Preface

While it is well-established that founders influence strategies and performance in young companies, little is known about the influence of founders' immigrant status on the early internationalization or the survival and growth of new high technology ventures. Traditionally, it has been assumed that immigrant entrepreneurs are disadvantaged relative to local entrepreneurs because they have limited access to resources and markets in their country of adoption. In this study, I draw on the concept of the *outsider*, which has both positive and negative connotations, to assess the advantages and disadvantages faced by immigrant entrepreneurs.

By drawing on the behavioral theory of the firm, I argue that although outsider status of entrepreneurs may convey some disadvantages domestically, this very status may serve both as a spur to encourage international efforts and insights to allow such efforts to flourish. In the empirical analyses, I use the Kauffman Firm Survey on newly founded high technology ventures in the U.S. My results show that new high-tech ventures with outsider founders are more likely to internationalize early, but somewhat surprisingly, these international ventures are less likely to survive and grow relative to their native-founded counterparts that have internationalized. This suggests that immigrant entrepreneurs tend to be overconfident in their own ability to internationalize successfully.

Acknowledgements

I would like to express my deepest gratitude to Prof. Harry Sapienza for his innumerable lessons and insights to make me a better writer. I would like to express my sincere appreciation to Prof. Sri Zaheer for her valuable support and encouragement. I extend many thanks to Leo Balk of LFB Scholarly as well as the series editors for this opportunity. I would like to greatly acknowledge and thank Kaufmann Foundation for providing financial support and the quantitative data for this study. I would also like to thank those entrepreneurs who accepted to interview with me and provided the qualitative data for this study.

I would like to thank my mother. In the absence of my father, the endless love, guidance, encouragement, and support she has given me made this book possible. I also would like to thank my sister and my borther-in-law.

Last, but not the least, I would like to thank my husband, Feza Isiklar, who always supports me.

CHAPTER 1
An Introduction: Outsider Entrepreneurs, Firm Strategy and Performance

With the globalization of the world economy, internationalization as a growth strategy is becoming more relevant for established companies and new ventures alike. Although scholars traditionally have focused on large, well-established firms to study internationalization, with the increasing prominence of the international new ventures in the world economy, internationalization of young and small companies are also receiving more interest (e.g. Oviatt & McDougall, 1994; Autio, Sapienza, & Almeida, 2000; Zahra, 2005). Yet, we still know very little about new venture internationalization even though new ventures face even greater challenges than established companies in international markets (Zahra, 2005). In this book, I examine how entrepreneurs' decisions to internationalize early are affected by their immigrant status, and the performance outcomes of this choice in terms of firm survival and growth in high technology industries.

Immigrant entrepreneurship (IE) research is built on idea that immigrant and native entrepreneurs do not compete on an equal footing (Light, 1979). IE scholars have argued that immigrant entrepreneurs are largely disadvantaged in the mainstream economy relative to native entrepreneurs because immigrant entrepreneurs suffer from the unfamiliarity with local economic, social, legal, and cultural circumstances, limited local information networks, and absence of effective relations with local governments, nationalistic costumers, and suppliers (Collins & Low, 2010). Building on these arguments, some researchers have empirically examined the influence of founders' immigrant status on firm performance and found that immigrant-founded new ventures often perform worse relative to native-founded new ventures (e.g. Vinogradov & Isaksen, 2008).

While this research has increased our understanding of immigrant entrepreneurs and their ventures, its main focus has been the immigrant entrepreneurs in low-growth industries and on the *disadvantages* that immigrant entrepreneurs face. That is, the IE literature has primarily tried to understand the *drawbacks* of outsiderness; especially focusing on how immigrant entrepreneurs face discrimination in the main stream economy and thus self-select themselves into self-employment, and how their ventures were unable to grow (Bates, 1997, Fairlie & Meyer, 1996). In this study, I take a behavioral theory approach and consider outsiderness not necessarily a disadvantage but an important factor that shapes founders' cognitions and their strategic choices. I use the terms "native" or "insider" to refer to a founder born in the country, in which the new venture is started, and "immigrant" or "outsider" to refer to a founder who was born outside that country. *"Outsider"* refers to a founder starting a new business in a country other than his or her country of origin[1].

Studying the impact of founders' outsider status on high-tech new ventures' international strategies and performance is timely given two recent trends. The first trend is an increase in the number of newly established high technology firms pursuing internationalization at their founding or very shortly thereafter (Shrader, Oviatt, & McDougall, 2000). These firms are shown to transfer technologies and managerial practices across international borders, innovate, create jobs, and eventually contribute to the development and growth of their countries at rates higher than entrepreneurial firms in general (Hessels & Stel, 2007). Although the challenges of internationalization are particularly salient for young companies, we know little about why these ventures

---

[1] In this study, "outsider" refers to those founders who started their independent new ventures in the US but were born in countries outside of the U.S.

internationalize, or how they overcome their liabilities of newness and foreignness despite their small size and limited resources (Zahra, 2005). The second trend is an increase in the number of new high technology companies founded by highly skilled immigrant entrepreneurs (Wadhwa, Rissing, Saxenian, & Gereffi, 2007). Immigrant-founded high technology startups accounted for more than 25.3 % of all high-growth companies started in the US from 1995 to 2005 (Wadhwa et al., 2007). We know very little about these newly emerging highly educated, high technology immigrants and their startups (Bhide, 2008; Kalnins & Chung, 2006). The work of Anne Le Saxenian is an exception to this (e.g. Saxenian, 1999; Saxenian & Hsu, 2001), but the main focus of her work has been the development of Silicon Valley and not the strategies or performance of immigrant-founded new ventures relative to their native counterparts in high technology sectors.

In order to increase our understanding of immigrant versus native entrepreneurs and the type of high technology companies that they develop, I examine the influence of founders' immigrant status on the internationalization strategies and performance of high technology new ventures. The gist of my inquiry surrounds how outsiderness will affect both the choice of whether or not to internationalize a high technology new venture early on, and the outcomes of such choices on the firm survival and growth for both immigrant-founded and native-founded new ventures. Being *"outsiders,"* immigrant entrepreneurs have less experiential knowledge and social embeddedness in their adopted country relative to native entrepreneurs (Hart, Acs, & Tracy, 2009, Shane, 2007). Traditionally, these differences are assumed to disadvantage immigrant-founded new ventures relative to native-founded new ventures by limiting their access to resources and markets in their country of adoption (Rath & Kloosteman, 2000; Dana, 1997). I argue that although highly skilled immigrant entrepreneurs also face some of these disadvantages in their country of adoption, this very status may provide them with the ability and the motivation to undertake early internationalization. For example, outsider founders, potentially free of cognitive and relational barriers, may be able to develop international business competencies that native entrepreneurs cannot easily replicate. Further, their early life experiences with personal mobility may incline them to build new ventures that are less locationally bound and have wider geographical market scope. In short, I ask the following questions in the context of high technology industries:

1. How does outsiderness versus insiderness (i.e., founders' immigrant status) affect early internationalization?
2. How does early internationalization affect firm survival and firm growth?
3. How does outsiderness versus insiderness (i.e., founders' immigrant status) affect firm survival and firm growth for domestic-only and international new ventures?

The challenge to answering these questions is finding an empirical setting with a large number of new ventures in high technology industries. Moreover, these ventures should be comparable in age, and vary in terms of characteristics of their owners (i.e., immigrant versus native) and their international strategies (i.e., domestic-only versus international). The Kaufmann Firm Survey (KFS) is an ideal data set that meets these requirements. KFS is a large panel data set of new businesses that were all founded in 2004 in the US. The data set consists of four follow up surveys (of the same firms) taking place in 2005, 2006, 2007, 2008 respectively. Because KFS follows the same cohort of firms over time, it helps to address the problems of reverse causation and survivor bias.

In order to have a deeper understanding of immigrant versus native-founded high technology new ventures and the strategies that they implement, I have also conducted *semi*-structured interviews with five immigrant and five native high-tech entrepreneurs. These interviews aimed at enriching my theoretical understanding (Yin, 2002), which then are quantitatively tested on KFS data set. And also, they serve to aid in interpreting the results of my quantitative analysis and shed a better light on some of the findings.

Early internationalization is an important strategy for new ventures to achieve competitiveness, innovativeness and success in today's global economy (Gupta, Govindarajan & Wang, 2008). However, it is also a risky strategy and not all new ventures might

Introduction

implement it equally successfully. Therefore, understanding the costs and benefits, causes and consequences of early internationalization is essential for entrepreneurs in deciding whether it is a right strategy for them. This research aims to inform potential insider and outsider entrepreneurs in taking the right steps in this regard. Also, given that many governments are promoting exports of technology and services in order to strengthen their national trade balances and increase their world market shares in critical industries, this study has implications for national governments in promoting international entrepreneurial firms, and for policy makers in devising immigration policies and entrepreneurial programs directed at immigrant-founded and native-founded high technology ventures.

The remainder of this book proceeds as follows: Chapter 2 and Chapter 3, I review the literature that relates to early internationalization and immigrant entrepreneurship and that provides foundation for this research. Based on the gaps that I identify in these literatures, in Chapter 4, I develop hypotheses about early internationalization and new venture performance as affected by founders' immigrant status. I draw on the behavioral theory of the firm to develop my hypotheses. In Chapter 5, I describe the methods in detail, including the sample, the data and variable construction, and the analysis techniques to test the hypotheses developed in Chapter 4. In Chapter 6, I provide results of the empirical analyses. In Chapter 7, I provide my impressions of the qualitative interviews that I conducted with immigrant and native entrepreneurs. In Chapter 8, I consider alternative explanations for my empirical results and reflect on the meaning of my results. Finally, in Chapter 9, I conclude with the theoretical and practical implications of my overall findings, limitations and possible future directions.

CHAPTER 2
Early Internationalization as a Firm Strategy

Studies show that firms pursue internationalization strategies at increasingly earlier ages than they have historically (Shrader, Oviatt & McDougall, 2000). According to statistics, small enterprises made up 97 % of all identified exporters and produced 31 % of the known export value in the US in 2008, and the majority of these companies are less than ten years old (U.S. Census Bureau, 2010). Although no universally accepted name or definition exists for these companies yet, the practical significance of the phenomenon and the scholarly attention given to it is increasing.

The ventures engaged in early internationalization have been referred to as "international new ventures" (Oviatt & McDougall, 1994), "born globals," "global startups" (Knight & Cavusgil, 1996), "instant internationals" (Preece, Miles, & Baetz, 1999), and "infant multinationals" (Rasmussen & Madsen, 2002). There are really no clearly articulated distinctions between these concepts. One of the most commonly used definitions for international new ventures is offered by Oviatt & McDougall (1994:49) as

> Business organizations that from inception seek to derive significant competitive advantage from the use of resources and the sale of outputs in multiple countries.

The interpretation of this definition varies significantly among researchers; many researchers have traditionally considered internationalizing small and medium size enterprises (SMEs) within the category of international new ventures although SMEs may not necessarily be young when they first enter international markets. However, this tradition seems to be changing in recent years with more research emphasis given to the timing of the internationalization rather than the size of the venture (DeClerq, Sapienza, Yavuz, & Zhou, 2012).

Moreover, researchers used different time frames as a criterion to empirically operationalize international new ventures (INVs) as a distinct organizational form[2]. For example, some researchers defined INVs as firms that began exporting at the outset (e.g. Knight & Cavusgil, 2004) while some others used two-year definition (e.g. McKinsey & Company, 1993; Knight & Cavusgil, 1996), three-year definition (e.g., Kummerle, 2002; Madsen & Knudse, 2003; Knight & Cavusgil, 2004), and six-year definition (e.g. Zahra, Ireland & Hitt, 2000; Yeoh, 2004; Fernhaber, McDougall & Shepherd, 2009). McDougall, Shane & Oviatt (1994) used an eight-year definition and some other researchers suggest that INVs are firms that enter foreign markets between two and six years after their establishment (e.g. Coviello & Munro, 1995).

International new ventures exist in large numbers not only in the U.S. but also in many other developed and developing economies, such as New Zealand (Coviello, 2006), Australia (Freeman & Cavusgil, 2007), Greece, Finland, Italy, Norway (Gabrielsson, Kirpalani, Dimitratos, Solberg, & Zucchella, 2008), Mexico (Hughes, Martin, Morgan, Robson, 2010), China, India, South Africa (Wood, Khavul,

---

[2] Some researchers also considered international sales intensity together with speed of internationalization to define international new ventures. For example, Knight & Cavusgil (1996) defined INVs as firms with a share of foreign sales of at least 25% and having foreign operations within two years after inception. For Madsen & Knudse (2003), INVs have more than 25% of foreign sales outside of their own continent within the first three years of their existence. And, Luostarien & Gabrielsson (2004) defined INVs as firms that enter global markets at the outset and have at least 50% of their sales outside of home continent.

Perez-Nordtvedt, Prakhya, Velarde & Zheng, 2011), France (Cabrol & Nlemvo, 2009), and U.K. (Cirk, 2010).

The increasing prevalence of INVs in the world economy requires new theorizing about the existence of INVs as a distinct organizational form (Madsen & Knudsen, 2003). While most early International Business (IB) theories predict a slow and incremental process of internationalization (e.g. Johanson & Vahlne, 1977), new ventures significantly deviate from such prototypes. These new ventures focus on speed and internationalize various value chain activities very early on, use a variety of entry modes, and enter and operate in various countries at once (Aspelund, Madsen & Moen, 2007).

Below, I will first review the international business literature as it relates to the process of internationalization. Next, I will review the international entrepreneurship literature on early internationalization, which developed as a response to the need for new theorizing about new venture internationalization.

International Business
International business (IB) research is built on the core idea that domestic and foreign firms are different (Hymer, 1976). Foreign firms are disadvantaged relative to domestic firms because they have to incur additional costs of overcoming unfamiliarity with local economic, social, legal, and cultural circumstances, newly creating local information networks, and establishing relations with local governments, nationalistic costumers, and suppliers (Miller & Richards, 2002; Zaheer & Mosakowski, 1997). Building on these arguments, researchers have empirically examined the influence of foreignness on firm performance (Eden & Miller, 2004; Zaheer, 1995) and found that these costs -also called liabilities of foreignness (LOF)- do exist and that they can negatively affect firm survival and financial performance (e.g. Insch & Miller, 2005; Mezias, 2002; Zaheer & Mosakowsi, 1997).

Therefore, if firms are going to internationalize successfully, they may need certain other advantages over domestic firms in order to thrive. International business research has tried to identify what these advantages are, how and why firms internationalize, and what value is created as a result of internationalization (Buckley, 2002). Several theories have been developed to address these questions. However, a dominant characteristic of these theories has been their orientation toward large well-established firms with an already strong domestic presence (Dana, Etemad & Wright, 1999). Therefore, the bulk of research in this literature overlooks the entrepreneurial and managerial aspects of internationalization that are especially pertinent to new ventures (Buckley & Lessard, 2005).

For example, in their review of these theories in an attempt to understand international new ventures, McDougall, Shane and Oviatt (1994) demonstrated the need for new theories to explain new venture internationalization. They argued that monopolistic advantage theory cannot explain early internationalization because the theory assumes that firms internationalize in order to exploit their domestically developed superior assets over local firms in foreign markets. However, new ventures internationalize before they develop superiority or monopolistic advantage at home. Similarly, product life cycle theory cannot explain internationalization of new ventures because the theory assumes that firms internationalize to capture new markets for their products that no longer have demand in domestic markets. However, new ventures may internationalize long before their domestic markets are saturated. McDougall et al (1994) argue that oligopolistic reaction theory also fails to explain early internationalization because the theory assumes that firms internationalize in order to match the actions of other members in an oligopoly. However, new ventures are often the first movers in an industry to internationalize their products abroad. In addition, internalization theory assumes that firms internationalize for efficiency reasons, and choose the lowest cost mode of international entry. However, international new ventures do not usually follow the lowest cost mode of entry and tend to use hybrid structures (Zacharakis, 1997).

Finally, the stage theory of internationalization- (Johanson & Vahlne, 1977), theorizes that firms internationalize in stages in order to decrease the uncertainty associated with foreign markets. In this theory, firms commit to foreign markets only incrementally in order to make sure that if something goes wrong, they can easily recover from it. Given that internationalization is a risky strategy, firms commit more resources to a market only after they gain enough experiential knowledge about it. Therefore, stage theory of internationalization predicts that firms accumulate enough resources, knowledge, and experiences before entering foreign markets. Moreover, they enter foreign markets in stages, that is, as they learn about a specific market, they gradually progress through no regular export, export through agents, direct exporting, licensing, joint ventures, and wholly owned subsidiaries. Finally, they also enter culturally familiar countries first, and then expand gradually into countries that are culturally less familiar (Johanson & Vahlne, 1977). However, this logic of internationalization also falls short of explaining the behaviors of many young and small firms that internationalize very rapidly and aggressively before accumulating necessary resources. These new ventures do not necessarily enter into countries that are culturally familiar first, nor do they conform to a single model of market entry (Burgel & Murray, 2000; Bell, 1995).

Summary
Early IB theorizing fails to explain internationalization of new ventures. This literature focuses on large multinational companies and makes assumptions that are not necessarily true for new ventures. New ventures are smaller and more resource constrained relative to established companies, making many traditional IB theories (e.g. oligopolistic reaction theory, internalization theory) fundamentally irrelevant for new venture internationalization. Moreover, entrepreneurs are the single most important element in new venture internationalization, while mangers of large established companies do not enjoy the same level of influence in internationalization decisions of their companies. The neglect of managerial characteristics in the traditional IB literature, therefore, limits its power in explaining new venture internationalization. So, the questions remain to be answered in this literature are: *What explains new venture internationalization? What is the role of the entrepreneurs in internationalization processes of new ventures?*

International Entrepreneurship
The limitations of traditional international business theories explaining the phenomenon of early internationalization have led later researchers

to begin to focus on the distinctive nature of new venture internationalization. This new stream of research builds on a pivotal article by Oviatt & McDougall (1994) on international new ventures. The fundamental research question in this literature is: Given that international business is risky even for established companies, why, how and with what outcomes do new ventures internationalize rather than operating solely in their home countries?

On the surface, this literature highlights some of the fundamental developments that have given rise to international new ventures. These developments are (a) changing market conditions such as specialization and homogenization of markets, and decreasing government protections that increased the number of global niche markets available to entrepreneurs, (b) technological developments in production, communication, and transportation that have made the access to international markets quicker, easier, and more convenient, (c) increased capabilities (i.e. education, knowledge, and international experiences) of entrepreneurs who are able to exploit international opportunities (Madsen & Servais, 1997; Etemad, 2004; Rialp, Rialp & Knight, 2005).

Although recent economic, political, technological, and social changes might provide a fertile ground for the emergence of international new ventures and help make early internationalization a rewarding strategy, challenges of internationalization for young companies still exist. In that sense, early internationalization is *"double-edged sword"* (Gupta, Govindarajan & Wang, 2008:221). Therefore, to theorize about INVs, it is important first to understand the benefits and risks associated with early internationalization.

Benefits of Early Internationalization
There are many potential benefits of early internationalization for young companies. First, internationalization provides new ventures with enormous potential for growth. Each foreign market provides an additional source of revenues. When a company starts operating internationally, it becomes part of the global market, expands its customer base, and this brings about better potential for long term growth. Second, selling in larger volumes increases the negotiation power of purchasing higher volumes of raw materials, increases

economies of scale, and thus, reduces fixed costs in production, and as a result increases profits. Third, by internationalizing, new ventures avoid dependency on domestic markets, and this lack of dependency on a single market ameliorates the effects of revenue fluctuations due to the fluctuations in domestic business cycles. Finally, operating internationally, new ventures gain various knowledge and experiences such as information on new technologies, new product and marketing ideas. This knowledge helps new ventures become more innovative and competitive in both domestic and international markets (Gupta, Govindarajan & Wang, 2008).

Costs of Early Internationalization
Internationalization is a costly and a risky strategy especially for new ventures with limited human, financial and reputational resources, or *"liabilities of newness."* First, entrepreneurs need to devote considerable time, money and effort to overcome the unfamiliarity with the economic, social, legal, and cultural circumstances of the foreign markets, and customize their products according to local needs. Even though the firm might be selling a universal product, it still incurs the costs of developing new promotional material, translating the labels on packaging into other foreign languages, newly creating local information networks. Second, entrepreneurs have to allocate key personnel and other critical resources from domestic activities to international ones such as international traveling, obtaining special international licenses, and keeping track of the foreign operations. Third, managing communication and coordination across borders is a difficult and costly task. Managing misunderstandings and inefficiencies across borders requires additional time and effort from managers. To sum up, new ventures already suffering from "liabilities of newness" face with these additional risks when they engage in early internationalization.

Given its risks, costs and benefits, early internationalization is an important decision that new ventures have to make. In trying to help this decision, researchers have examined various individual /entrepreneur-specific, firm-specific, and environment-specific factor that lead to early internationalization, and the financial and non-financial firm-level outcomes of this decision.

Antecedents of Early Internationalization
Antecedents of early internationalization can be divided into three subcategories. These are environment-specific, firm-specific, and individual /entrepreneur-specific factors (Hessels, 2008; Zahra & George, 2002).

The Role of Environment-Specific Factors:
Environment specific factors relate to characteristics (characteristics of home country, and host countries) and industry conditions in which new ventures operate.

Country Factors. Home country factors are also referred to as "country push factors" because these factors push new ventures to look for opportunities outside their home countries. One of the most important country-push factors is small market size. Not having enough customers to serve in their home countries, new ventures search for new markets very early in their lives (Fan & Phan, 2007; Rasmussan, Madsen & Evangelista, 2001; Madsen & Servais, 1997). Intensity of the domestic competition (Fan & Phan, 2007), limited availability of resources such as raw materials (Etemad, 2004) and high production costs (Axinn, 1988) are among other home country push factors identified in the literature that force new ventures to look for opportunities in other countries. Studies also show that the degree of the internationalization of other firms in the new ventures' home country also affects early internationalization by putting isomorphic pressures on new ventures to internationalize (Fernhaber & Li, 2010).

Host country related factors, also called country-pull factors, includes liberalization of markets (Acs, Morck, Shaver & Yeung, 1997), availability of advanced communication technologies (Knight & Cavusgil, 1996), globalization of customer needs, supplies, and value chain activities, availability of needed resources such as availability of financing and raw materials (Etemad, 2004), and the similarity of foreign markets to the domestic one (Madsen, Rasmussen, & Servais, 2000).

Industry Factors. A significant majority of the studies in the international entrepreneurship literature examined internationalization of new ventures in high technology industries, arguing that the effects of globalization and technological developments are most strongly felt

Early Internationalization

in high technology industries (e.g. Oviatt & McDougall, 1994; McKinzey and Co, 1993). For example, Shrader, Oviatt & McDougall (2000) examined 212 foreign market entries by 87 new ventures and showed that four industry characteristics, namely the degree of global integration, the speed of technological change, the degree of domestic competition, and the rate of industry growth, have a positive effect on early internationalization. In support of this finding, Andersson, Gabrielsson & Wictor (2004) also showed that early internationalization is more common when the industry is growing, and technological change is faster, confirming that new ventures in high technology industries tend to internationalize earlier.

The Role of Firm-Specific Factors:
Mostly within the context of high technology industries, scholars also examined several firm characteristics affecting early internationalization. These studies largely focused on product characteristics, niche strategies, strategic orientations, and social networks. These studies found that new ventures with high quality, innovative and highly differentiated global products (Knight & Cavusgil, 2004), narrow and clearly defined set of competencies (Nummela et al., 2004), learning orientation (Burpitt & Rondinelli, 2000), entrepreneurial orientation (Cavusgil & Knight, 2009), market orientation (Knight and Cavusgil 2004), experiential know-how including the presence of strong trademarks, brands, or industry specific know-how (Tuppura, 2008), niche market strategies (Almor, 2000; Rasmussen & Madsen, 2002; Rennie, 1993), marketing competence (Knight & Cavusgil, 2004), international networks (Casillas et al., 2009; Coviello & Munro, 1995), and foreign alliances and collaborative partnerships (Schwens & Kabst, 2009b) tend to internationalize earlier in their life cycles.

For example, Knight & Servais (2003) surveyed 186 and 106 international new ventures from the U.S. and Denmark, respectively, and showed that product quality, marketing competence, and product differentiation were the key competences of international new ventures that made them unique in their market space, and prevented head to head competition with other firms in foreign markets. In their in-depth case studies with four high technology new ventures, Coviello &

Munro (1995) showed that new ventures' international networks helped them develop their international markets quickly by providing them access to and information about foreign markets.

The Role of Individual/ Entrepreneur-Specific Factors:
Individual specific factors relates to characteristics of entrepreneur. In their conceptual article, Servais & Madsen (1997:567) stated that:

> In order to fully understand this phenomenon [early internationalization] we have to examine the background of the founders. In the case of born globals we may assume that background of the decision maker (founder) has a large influence on the internationalization path followed. Factors like education, experience from living abroad, experience from other internationally oriented jobs, etc. mould the mind of the founder and decrease the psychic distances to specific product markets significantly.

This suggests that some entrepreneurs may not see national borders as a barrier, but an opportunity to be exploited (Servais & Madsen, 1997). Consequently, researchers examined several entrepreneurial characteristics facilitating or inhibiting early internationalization. For example, researchers found that younger age (Andersson, Gabrielsson & Wictor, 2004), higher educational attainment (Federico, Kantis, Rialp, Rialp, 2009), entrepreneurial vision (Oviatt & McDougall, 1994), international experience (Kuemmerle, 2002), global mindset (Freeman & Cavusgil, 2007), personal networks at home and abroad (Harris & Wheeler, 2005), and prior international and technological knowledge (Nordman & Melen, 2008) positively affects early internationalization.

For example, by examining 61 venture capital backed companies, Bloodgood, Sapienza & Almeida (1997) found that international work experince of top managers positively related to the extent of early internationalization. They argued that international experiences incerase awareness of the foreign opportunities and facilitate early internationalization. Likewise, in their qualitative study of nine Australian new ventures, Freeman & Cavusgil (2007) showed that the global mindset and the international networks of entrepreneurs has an important positive influence on new ventures' early commitment to international markets. Surprisingly, few studies examined the role of founders' immigrant status as an important driver of early internationalization, except for a few articles that mentioned its relevance. In one example, by analyzing 24 high - tech new ventures, McDougall et al. (1994) reported that "...*the founders of international new ventures were often immigrants and had family and personal contacts overseas.*" *(pp. 479).* However, no theoretical explanation was offered in the paper nor has additional research been conducted to understand this finding. Our theoretical and empirical understanding regarding how entrepreneurs' immigrant status affects the internationalization of their ventures is very limited although foreign born entrepreneurs play increasingly significant roles in high technology entrepreneurship and understanding this relationship might provide new insights why firms differ in their international strategies and performance (Hart et. al., 2009).

Outcomes of Early Internationalization
Studies on the outcomes of early internationalization are much more limited than the studies on antecedents (Zahra, 2005; Keupp & Gassmann, 2009). Moreover, these studies almost exclusively examined firm-level outcomes of early internationalization, and largely overlooked the influence of early internationalization on individual–level outcomes (e.g., entrepreneurs' human capital, satisfaction, health) and macro-level outcomes (e.g., employment growth, innovation, economic growth) with few exceptions (e.g. Stam, Suddle, Hessel & Stel, 2009; Hessel & van Steel, 2008).

Firm level outcomes of early internationalization can be financial or non-financial. Researchers examining the financial consequences of early internationalization have studied firm survival (Mudambi & Zahra, 2007), sales growth (Zahra et. al, 2000), international sales growth (Zhou, Barnes & Lu, 2010; Autio, Sapienza & Almeida, 2000), profitability (Fernhaber & Li, 2010, Zhou, Wu & Luo, 2007), return on equity (ROE) (Zahra et. al, 2000), return on asset (ROI) (McDougall & Oviatt, 2005). Some of these studies used hard performance figures (Fernhaber & Li, 2010) while others used entrepreneurs' perceptions of performance (e.g. Yeoh, 2004). These studies are still few in number, and produced largely contradictory and inconclusive results.

For example, by studying 59 entrepreneurial electronic firms in Finland, Autio, Sapienza & Almeida (2000) concluded that the earlier new ventures internationalize, the higher their international sales growth. On the other hand,, Mudambi & Zahra (2007) studied 275 British international new ventures and showed that after controlling for competitive strategies, early internationalization had no effect on firm survival. Moreover, Sapienza et al. (2006) theoretically argued that early internationalization negatively affects firm survival while it also increases the room for growth. However, very few studies have simultaneously examined different performance dimensions of early internationalization. One of the exceptions is Carr, Haggard, Hmieleski & Zahra (2010), who examined a longitudinal sample of 787 firms and concluded that while early internationalization had a positive effect on short-term growth, its effect of firm survival was inconclusive.

As for non-financial outcomes, researchers studied future internationalization intent (Casillas, Navarro & Sapienza, 2010), organizational learning (Schwens & Kabst, 2009a), employment growth (Westhead, Wright & Ucbasaran, 2001), technological competence (Knight & Cavusgil, 2004). For example, by studying 312 independent and corporate new ventures, Zahra, Ireland, & Hitt (2000) showed that international diversity of new ventures positively affected their technological learning, Moreover, Sapienza, De Clercq, and Sandberg (2005) asserted that early involvement with internationalization positively affected their international learning.

Summary
The primary focus of international entrepreneurship literature is the causes and consequences of early internationalization. Surprisingly however, although internationalization is about crossing borders, current research has not examined whether people who have already crossed borders also become international entrepreneurs, whether there is a difference between immigrant and native-founded new ventures in their propensity to internationalize early, and whether having crossed borders before as an entrepreneur has a differential effect on the successes of domestic versus international new ventures. So, the

question remains to be answered in this literature are: *Whether and how founders' immigrant status affects early internationalization and performance of new ventures in high technology industries?*

CHAPTER 3
Immigrant Entrepreneurship (IE) and a Conceptual Clarification: Outsider versus Insider Entrepreneurs

Immigrant or outsider entrepreneurs and their ventures have been examined in a separate literature called immigrant entrepreneurship. Most studies in this literature examined the reasons why immigrants start companies in their adopted countries, what industries they operate in and how their businesses perform. Although the focus has traditionally been on low-skilled immigrants and their businesses, in recent years researchers have begun to study high-tech/high skilled immigrant entrepreneurs. The following sub-sections provide a summary of this literature under three categories: (1) Research on the selection of immigrants into self-employment; (2) Research on the low-tech immigrant entrepreneurship; and (3) Recent research on high-tech immigrant entrepreneurship.

Selection of Immigrants into Self-Employment
The bulk of the research on immigrant entrepreneurship has focused on the factors that lead immigrants to engage in self-employment in their adopted countries. Studies have found that lack of attractive opportunities due to discrimination in the mainstream economy was the

main reason why immigrants start new businesses (Aldrich & Waldinger, 1990). By integrating prior work, Dana (1997) offers a model of self-employment by immigrants and suggests that both the entrepreneurial culture of the ethnic communities and the culture of the host societies are important in driving self-employment decision of immigrants. Specifically, she argues that immigrants from those ethnic communities that value entrepreneurship are more likely to become entrepreneurs. Moreover, she argues that the higher the sense of separateness from the rest of the host society, and the more immigrants' awareness of deprivation and diminished social status in the host country, the more likely immigrants will go into self-employment to compensate for their disadvantages in the labor market and diminished social status in the host country.

For example, Aldrich, Cater, Jones & McEvoy (1981) examined 600 small retailers and found that a large portion of Asian shopkeepers were more qualified compared with native shopkeepers but they were pushed into self-employment because of the unemployment, poverty, and discrimination that they faced in their adopted country. The study concluded that the lack of opportunities in the labor market for paid jobs was the primary reason for self-employment among Asian immigrants.

Recent studies have also examined the self employment decisions of highly skilled immigrants into self-employment. This research argues that "the glass ceiling" that highly skilled immigrants face in the corporate world motivates them to go to self-employment (Saxenian, 2002). For example, Lofstrom (2002) used data from the 1980 and 1990 U.S. Censuses to analyze the labor market experience of high-skilled immigrants relative to high-skilled natives, and concluded that predicted earnings of self-employed immigrants were estimated to be higher throughout most of their work life relative to wage/salary immigrants as well as compared to self-employed natives. Moreover, Saxenian (1999) studied highly skilled entrepreneurs and she attributed the high percentage of startups established by immigrant entrepreneurs in Silicon Valley to "the glass ceiling" that immigrants face with within their existing employers.

Low Skill /Low-Tech Immigrant Entrepreneurship

The traditional literature in immigrant entrepreneurship has largely focused on low-tech industries when examining the businesses started by immigrant entrepreneurs. This research argues that low skilled immigrants are naturally restricted to low growth sectors such as ethnic food or garments, and they rely on people in their marginalized ethnic networks for financing, advice, employees, and customers (Wilson and Portes, 1980). This isolation from the rest of the society, their limited fluency in the adopted country's language and their limited knowledge about the adopted country's formal and informal institutions were among the most important reasons why these businesses' growth was limited (Iyer & Shapiro, 1999).

For example, Chaganti and Greene (2002) examined 112 immigrant entrepreneurs of Latino and Asian origin and found that immigrants who were highly involved with their ethnic communities founded businesses that functioned in relative isolation from the mainstream economy, and these companies were smaller and had less positive cash flows. Moreover, the personal backgrounds of highly ethnically involved entrepreneurs were significantly weaker such that they had fewer years of work experience and education in the U.S.

Other studies examined differences within immigrant communities and the role of cultural values in explaining the successful creation and growth of businesses across different immigrant communities. For example, Morris & Schindehutte (2005) examined first generation entrepreneurs from six ethnic groups within the state of Hawaii: Japanese, Korean, Filipino, Chinese, Vietnamese, and Native Hawaiian, and concluded that while some values such as honesty and ambition were common to all immigrant entrepreneurs, other values such as loyalty and duty were specific to certain ethnicities (e.g. Asian).

Some of this work also examined international activities of immigrant entrepreneurs. These studies have argued that having distinctive group attachments with people in their home countries, many immigrant entrepreneurs are able to sustain social relationships in two socially embedded environments, or transnational spaces, and able to acquire resources from their both home and host societies to set up and operate ethnic businesses in their adopted countries (Portes, 1995). For example, Portes, Guarnizo & Haller (2002) studied Colombian,

Dominican, and Salvadoran immigrant entrepreneurs who operate in low growth sectors such as construction, manufacturing, retail sales, and personal services in the U.S., and showed that married male immigrant entrepreneurs with larger home country networks were more likely to establish transnational enterprises that either obtained ethnic inputs from or sold outputs to immigrants' countries of origin. (Portes et al., 2002).

High Skill /High-Tech Immigrant Entrepreneurship

New highly skilled immigrants of recent years are likely to be quite different from low skilled immigrant entrepreneurs of most studies. The majority of them come to the US for higher education. Many of them earn masters and PhD degrees in science and technology fields from US universities, and work for US corporations before they start their own businesses (Economist, March 2009). These companies operate in high growth sectors such as semiconductors, software, biotechnology, and compete with firms founded by US entrepreneurs (Economist, March 2009).

Anne Saxenian (1999) pioneered research focusing on highly skilled immigrant entrepreneurs. She found that highly skilled immigrant entrepreneurs, especially Indian and Chinese, play increasingly important roles in the development of Silicon Valley. She found that almost 50 % of all businesses started in the Silicon Valley were started by an immigrant entrepreneur. More recent studies using nationally representative samples concluded that the shares of immigrant entrepreneurs in high technology new ventures are 25 % (Wadhwa et. al., 2007) and 16 % (Hart et. al., 2009).

Several studies by Saxenian and her colleagues also examined international activities of highly skilled immigrant entrepreneurs (e.g. Saxenian, 2006; Saxenian, 2002; Saxenian & Hsu, 2001). They have examined how immigrant entrepreneurs engage in international activities with their countries of origin and how they diffuse entrepreneurial orientations and practices around the world. For example, Saxenian & Hsu (2001) showed that the community of US-educated Taiwanese engineers and entrepreneurs in Silicon Valley has helped develop Taiwan's Hsinchu region by transferring of capital, skill, and knowledge to Taiwan. They concluded that highly skilled immigrant entrepreneurs are able to build long-distance bridges allowing them to benefit from the skills and resources of their home countries and Silicon Valley simultaneously, and to help contribute to the industrial upgrading in their countries of origin.

Summary

Research on immigrant entrepreneurship literature traditionally focused on selection of immigrants into self-employment and on low skilled immigrants and their ventures. Although some recent studies examining high-tech immigrant entrepreneurs have yielded some important insights about this new group of entrepreneurs, these studies have largely focused on macro level outcomes such as regional development. Therefore, our theoretical and empirical understanding of the influence of founders' outsider status on firm strategy and performance in high technology industries is very limited. So, the question that remains to be answered in this literature is: *How does founders' immigrant status affect international strategies and performance in high-technology industries?*

A Conceptual Clarification: Outsider versus Insider Entrepreneurs

I define immigrant or outsider entrepreneurs as *"people who were born as citizens of one country, and subsequently move to and found a new venture in another country at some point in their life time"* (Wadha et al., 2007. pp. 9). As this definition suggests unlike "insider" entrepreneurs, "outsider" entrepreneurs are foreign-born individuals. They do not belong to their adopted countries from the beginning through organic connections such as kinship or locality (Gudykunst, 1983). Their socialization takes place in their countries of origin with different cultures, languages, religions, and political, legal and economic systems. Although outsider entrepreneurs live in their country of adoption, because they are outsiders, it is difficult for them to be as socially embedded in their adopted country as are insider entrepreneurs.

First, immigrant entrepreneurs have limited knowledge about formal and informal institutions and specific business practices in their country of adoption relative to native entrepreneurs. Although their personal experiences prior to starting a new business may help bridge some of this gap, their proficiency in cultural and linguistic know-how including local habits, preferences, market structure and ways of approaching customers, knowledge of business models, and institutions would be still limited relative to native entrepreneurs. Immigrant entrepreneurs could obtain this specific knowledge only by operating in their adopted country experientially over time as they develop networks and connections. So, immigrant-founded new ventures suffer from this experiential knowledge gap especially in the first few years of their operations in their adopted countries.

Second, being outsiders, immigrant entrepreneurs have limited access to key networks in their country of adoption (Hart et al., 2009). Prior research shows that the extent of entrepreneurs' social networks, or trusting personal connections and relationships, affects new ventures' outcomes (Adler & Kwon, 2002). These outcomes are likely to result from different access to money, talent, contacts, and information about markets and technology (Gulati, Nohria, Zaheer, 2000). These networks also help new ventures establish credibility and legitimacy in domestic markets (Aldrich & Fiol, 1994). Because immigrant entrepreneurs are different from the rest of society in many respects including their countries of origin, language, culture, and life experiences, establishing trusting relationships and networks requires additional time and effort (Zaheer & Zaheer, 2006) Thus, immigrant-founded new ventures often suffer from limited social embeddedness especially in the first few years of their operations relative to native-founded new ventures.

Although in this study I define outsiderness as being outsider to the *country* in which an entrepreneur starts his business, *"outsiderness"* is a more general concept that can be defined and operationalize differently depending on a particular research context. An entity (e.g. a person, a firm, group of firms...etc.) may be outsider within the boundaries of a business organization, a business group or network, an industry, a city, a state or a country. In the strategic management literature, for example, a lot of attention has been devoted in understanding the performance consequences of having an outsider versus an insider CEO (e.g. see Zhang & Rajagopalan, 2010; Karaevli, 2007). In this literature, outsiderness is often defined as having little or no work experience and network relationships in a particular organization or in an industry. Similarly, in team literature, many studies have examined the implication of having outsider team members for various team outcomes such as productivity, efficiency and creativity. In these studies outsider team members are often defined as those who are not members of particular functional departments or professions (e.g. see Thompson & Choi, 2006).

International business literature has also given special importance to the concept of outsiderness along with the concept of foreignness. In this literature, foreignness and outsidership are defined slightly differently. Subsidiaries of corporations in host countries are described as *foreign* due to "their network positions in the host country and their linkages to important actors" as well as their "distance from cognitive, normative, and regulative domains of the local institutional environment…" (Zaheer, 2002: 351-352). On the other hand, Johanson & Vahlne (2009) have recently emphasized the role of insidership and outsidership in the process of internationalization. They (2009: 1415) define *outsidership* as *"a firm that does not have a position in a relevant network."* They argue that outsidership is a liability or an impediment while insidership is a necessary condition for successful internationalization because *"it is to a large extent via relationships firms learn, and build trust and commitment – the essential elements of the internationalization process (2009:1415)."*

I use the term *"outsiderness"* to refer to a founder starting a new business in a country other than his or her country of origin and assume that outsider entrepreneurs have more limited knowledge and social embeddedness in their country of adoption relative to insider entrepreneurs. It is important to note that *outsiderness* (and therefore *insiderness*) is not an absolute concept but it is a relative concept. In this study, understanding the influence of having an outsider entrepreneur for the strategies and performance of a new venture makes sense only when these influences are understood relative to having an insider entrepreneur and vice versa.

CHAPTER 4
Early Internationalization and Performance: Does Outsiderness Matter?

Internationalization into new markets is an entrepreneurial act, involving international opportunity recognition and exploitation processes (Chandra, Styles, Wilkinson, 2009). From a pure economic point of view where socially atomized individuals rationally pursue their maximum self-interests in the same market fields with perfect information, people and firms will discover the same international opportunities, or opportunities discovered will not be related to the personal or social attributes of the entrepreneurs, or the firm characteristics. That is, whether a firm is founded by an immigrant or not should not make any difference to a firm's international opportunity recognition and/or its exploitation.

However, we know from entrepreneurship research that because asymmetric information and subjective world views are necessary for opportunity identification (Kirzner, 1997), entrepreneurs' backgrounds, prior experiences, social relationships, and social contexts lead different entrepreneurs to pursue different entrepreneurial opportunities, form new ventures with different characteristics, and achieve different performance outcomes (Shane and Venkataraman, 2000, Shane, 2000). Therefore, founder characteristics have important implications for new venture internationalization and performance (Freeman & Cavusgil, 2007).

As a theory of decision making, the behavioral theory of the firm is a useful lens to understand how *outsiderness* (and for that matter *insiderness*) might affect entrepreneurs' cognitions and actions to internationalize early and how that decision drives firm performance in terms of survival and growth both for immigrant and native-founded high-tech new ventures.

Behavioral Theory of the Firm

Neoclassical economics has traditionally modeled human decision making based on the result of personal calculations of utility and cost. This tradition has assumed that each person knows all the possible alternatives, their costs, and his/her own utility function accurately. And, therefore individuals make the most optimal decision with perfect information. Among all alternatives, they choose the alternative that maximizes the benefit and/or minimizes the cost and over all maximizes their utility.

The behavioral theory of the firm (Cyert & March, 1963) has been developed as an alternative model this "rational man" model of classical economics. The theory disputes the economic theories' basic assumptions and asserts that people are not complicated machines that can calculate utility and cost accurately and make perfect decisions. Instead, the theory maintains that people are 1) boundedly rational, meaning people are limited in their attention spans, information processing capabilities, and foresight; 2) people are uncertainty avoiders, meaning that in uncertain situations, they rely on information that are familiar to them; and 3) they satisfice, meaning that people are content with finding a satisfactory solution rather the best solution (Bromiley, 2005). Simon (1997:8) asserts that:

> People have reasons for what they do, but these reasons depend very much on how people frame or represent the situations in which they find themselves, and on the information they have or obtain about variables that they take into account. Their rationality is a procedural rationality: there is no claim that they grasp the environment accurately

or comprehensively. To predict their behavior in specific instances, we must know what they are attending to and what information that they have.

In other words, when people or firms make decisions, they neither search for all available alternatives nor unfailingly select the best one. Instead, they search for solutions in the areas that are familiar to them, and when they satisfy, they stop the search (Bromiley, 2005). These satisficing solutions to the past problems then make up routines, or repertories of action, that firms in turn rely on for further decision making. To put it another way, how firms solved their problems in the past has implications for how they solve their problems in the future. In that sense, the theory asserts that firms are routine-based and path dependent. That is, history matters in a firm's strategic decisions.

Given that new ventures themselves do not have much history, the personal history of the founders, their life experiences, knowledge base and relationships become critical in guiding the ways new ventures look for, comprehend, evaluate, and apply new information to identify and exploit new opportunities (Bhide, 2000). Therefore, in order to hypothesize about the effect of outsiderness on new venture strategy and performance, we need to understand how outsider entrepreneurs differ from their insider counterparts in their personal histories and life experiences.

Outsider versus Insider Entrepreneurs and Early Internationalization

Highly skilled outsider entrepreneurs have tendencies and experiences that distinguish them from their insider counterparts. First, outsider entrepreneurs are people who have voluntarily decided to move abroad possibly in search of better opportunities. Leaving one's own country and living elsewhere is a risky action that is full of unknowns, and by the act of emigration, highly skilled outsider entrepreneurs demonstrate not only their higher cross-border opportunity seeking and risk taking propensities (Chaganti, Watts, Chaganti and Zimmerman-Treichel, 2008) but also their openness to divergent cultural experiences and institutional environments (Muzychenko, 2008). The experience of getting out of their comfort zone and spotting international opportunities for education or employment across borders may shape outsider entrepreneurs' subsequent search for cross border opportunities for future actions.

Moreover, moving from one country to another exposes outsider entrepreneurs to diverse cultural experiences and these experiences improve outsider entrepreneurs' ability for adaptation to unfamiliar settings. As a result, outsider entrepreneurs develop cross-cultural understandings, or a relatively more global mind set than native entrepreneurs (Herman & Smith, 2010). For example, in their empirical study of 65 managers in the textile industry, Arora, Jaju, Kefalas & Perenich (2004) show that managers' foreign country living experience and the existence of a family member from a foreign country have statistically significant positive impact on their global mindset. Global mindset involves cultural self-awareness and affects information-processing patterns by directing attention to diverse information about both domestic and international markets, facilitating international opportunity recognition and exploitation processes (Levy, Beechler, Taylor & Boyacigiller, 2007).

In contrast to outsider entrepreneurs, insider entrepreneurs are more likely to develop a domestic world view or domestic mindset. Not having the experience of moving to and starting a business in another country, and being rooted within their domestic contexts, insider entrepreneurs may have limited propensity to think "outside of the box," reducing their attention to international opportunities (Herman & Smith, 2010). Autio et al. (2000) refer to these limitations that occur due to the familiarity with domestic environment as "cognitive barriers." According to the authors, *cognitive barriers* arise because firms' existing domestic knowledge base and experiences and local understanding direct the subsequent search efforts and constrain the identification of opportunities in international markets. In line with this logic, for example, Levy (2005) studies 69 American firms and finds that firms are more likely to be global when their top management team pays attention to the global environment. Firms led by managers that pay more attention to the domestic environment are less likely to consider globalization as a viable strategic choice or to develop extensive global operations.

Not only their experience of cross-country mobility, but also the lack of strong roots or embeddedness in their countries of adoption inclines outsider entrepreneurs to build ventures that are more likely to be international at or near their foundings relative to insider entrepreneurs. Although the absence of strong domestic networks is a major disadvantage for outsider entrepreneurs since it limits their legitimacy, credibility, and access to resources relative their insider counter parts in their adopted county (Portes, 1995), limited social embeddedness also brings advantages to outsider entrepreneurs. The absence of strong ties and social constraints on outsider entrepreneurs free their boundaries to look for opportunities elsewhere. Herman and Smith (2010:170) state that:

> There are hardships of relocation but also the advantages that come to a stranger in a strange land. Freed from the constraints of culture and tradition, and may be judgmental peers, newcomers are free to express themselves. With independence come confidence, resourcefulness and creativity.

Moreover, prior research shows that given the difficulty of accessing key domestic social networks, outsider entrepreneurs tend to rely on their co-ethnic social and professional networks such as The Indus Entrepreneurs (TIE) for Indians, and Chinese Business Association for Chinese (Saxenian, 2006). These organizations function to fill the lack of social ties for outsider entrepreneurs, and connect them with each other (Saxenian, 2002). Moreover, research shows that non-nationals in a country identify and socialize with each other more than they do with nationals because of their out-group identity (i.e., all immigrants are outsiders regardless of their home country while all natives are insiders) (Yuki, 2003). This implies that immigrant entrepreneurs socialize with other ethnicities more than native entrepreneurs socialize with other ethnicities. This means that immigrant entrepreneurs have more opportunities to learn about other countries and cultures, and potential opportunities to do business with those countries than native entrepreneurs. Therefore, both their connections with people from several countries in their country of adoption facilitate the early internationalization for outsider entrepreneurs relative to their insider counterparts.

Furthermore, although the presence of domestic social networks might help insider entrepreneurs flourish domestically and help build domestic power bases, these strong ties such as family members, friends, relatives and colleagues also induce them to focus their energies and efforts on the domestic markets (Stam, 2007), limiting their propensity to pursue international opportunities. Autio et al. (2000) refer to this limitation occurring due to domestic social ties as "relational barriers." According to the authors *relational barriers* arise because existing domestic social networks create reciprocal loyalties and obligations and make it difficult for insider entrepreneurs to shift their attention and effort from domestic markets to international markets. For example, Bouquet (2005) finds empirical support for the hypothesis that the firms' decision environment influences attention structures, and their interest in global issues.

In summary, new ventures with outsider founders are less subject to cognitive and relational impediments to early internationalization relative to insider entrepreneurs. On the contrary, their experience of cross border mobility, limited social embeddeness in their adopted country and their openness to diverse cultural experiences allow them to be more willing and able to identify and exploit international opportunities earlier in their life cycles relative to insider entrepreneurs. This leads to the following hypotheses:

H1: Immigrant-founded new ventures are more likely to be international at or near their founding than are native-founded new ventures.

Early Internationalization and Firm Performance
Whether they are large MNEs or small new ventures, firms face several complexities and uncertainties in entering and operating in foreign markets. Eden & Miller (2004) suggest that costs of internationalization efforts can be categorized into two groups. These are *"Cost of Doing Business Abroad"* (CDBA) and *"Liabilities of Foreignness"* (LOF). According to the authors, CDBA are the economic costs including production, marketing and distribution costs that occur due to

geographic distance such as transportation and communications costs, trade barriers, and volatile exchange rates while LOF are the social costs that foreign firms face over and above those faced by domestic firms in a host country. The authors further decompose LOF into three types of costs: unfamiliarity, relational and discriminatory hazards that arise from the corresponding to the regulatory, normative, and cognitive institutional distance between countries. Unfamiliarity costs reflect lack of knowledge and experience about the local economic, social, legal, and cultural circumstances of the host country such as differing laws and regulations, languages and customs. Relational costs reflect managerial or administrative costs of organizing such as newly creating local information networks, and establishing and monitoring partnerships with local actors, or managing employees across borders. Finally, discriminatory costs reflect differential treatment by ethnocentric local governments, nationalistic costumers, and suppliers such as entry barriers created by host market firms, entry barriers created by host governments (Eden & Miller, 2004; Miller & Richards, 2002; Zaheer & Mosakowski, 1997).

Given that firms have to incur both CDBA and LOF when they internationalize, they often need to possess some excess resources so as to deal with the challenges of foreign markets, and insure the reliability of their performance. While large established firms might have more slack resources or excess capacity to deal with these challenges (Acs et al, 1997, Zacharakis, 1997), new ventures that also suffer from "liabilities of newness" (Stinchcome, 1965) face double liabilities in foreign markets. In particular, both their lack of external legitimacy, internal coordination, and their limited human and financial resources (Singh, Tucker & House, 1986) make it very difficult for new ventures to manage both domestic and foreign markets simultaneously (Etemad, 2004), and, thus, entailing these additional risks, internationalization threatens new ventures short-term survival. Therefore, current literature on early internationalization maintains that although early internationalization creates enormous growth opportunities in the long term, it also amplifies liabilities, and decreases the probability of a new venture's short term survival (Sapienza et al., 2006). This leads to the following hypothesis:

H2a: Early internationalization lowers the probability of new venture survival.

Although early internationalization is a very risky and costly strategy to implement, it might provide firms with additional growth opportunities. Internationalization provides new ventures with new markets, expands their customer bases, increases sales, and contributes to their long term performance. Moreover, international markets provide new ventures with diverse learning and continuous growth opportunities (De Clerq et al, 2013). During internationalization, new ventures gain various knowledge and experiences such as information on new technologies, new product and marketing ideas (De Clerq et al, 2013). This knowledge helps new ventures become more innovative and competitive both domestically and internationally.

Based on the behavioral theory of the firm (Levitt & March, 1988), prior research argues that because firm behavior is path dependent in the sense that a firm's past history as captured by routines influences what it does in the future, young firms with limited domestic routines may be free of domestic competency traps, or impediments to learning in international markets (Autio et al, 2000; Sapienza et al., 2006). Therefore, prior research argues that young ventures have "learning advantages of newness" and that they benefit from internationalization and achieve high degrees of growth (Autio et al, 2000; Sapienza et al., 2006).

For example, Autio et al (2000) studied 59 entrepreneurial electronic firms in Finland and concluded the earlier firms internationalize, the higher their international sales growth. Moreover, Carr, Haggard, Hmieleski & Zahra (2010), who examined a longitudinal sample of 787 firms and concluded that early internationalization had a positive effect on short-term growth. In summary, being quickly adoptable to new markets, new ventures can gain knowledge about foreign customers and competitors allowing them to modify their product features, to ensure quality, customer services and other activities, and as a result achieve higher rates of growth relative to new ventures with domestic sales only (Yeoh, 2004). This leads to the following hypothesis:

H2b: Conditional on survival, early internationalization increases the subsequent growth of new ventures in the short-run.

Outsider versus Insider Entrepreneurs, Early Internationalization and Firm Survival and Growth

I argue that the relationship between founders' immigrant status and the performance of the new ventures is not straightforward. That relationship depends on the strategy of the new venture such that while outsider entrepreneurs might face disadvantages in their adopted countries and perform worse relative to insider entrepreneurs, they might have advantages in international markets and perform better relative to insider entrepreneurs. These arguments are detailed below.

Immigrant-founded domestic-only new ventures in their country of adoption face similar disadvantages that international new ventures face when they enter new foreign markets. However, the distinction is that although an international new venture would face both costs of doing business abroad, (or the economic costs of internationalization), and liabilities of foreignness, (or the social costs of internationalization), an immigrant-founded domestic-only new venture would incur only liabilities of foreignness because having been started and operated in the adopted country, immigrant-founded domestic-only ventures would not incur additional economic costs arising from geographic distance while they would still incur social costs arising from unfamiliarity, relational and discriminatory hazard in the county of adoption. Therefore, in comparison to native-founded domestic-only ventures, immigrant-founded domestic-only ventures would face greater disadvantages and perform worse relative to native-founded new ventures.

Prior work also shows that because immigrant-founded new ventures suffer from the outsider status in their country of adoption, they are disadvantaged relative to their native counterparts in accessing domestic opportunities, resources, and legitimacy. For example, Vinogradov & Isaken (2008) examined a longitudinal sample of 389 domestic ventures in Norway and concluded survival rate is lower for businesses established by immigrant entrepreneurs compared to those established by native entrepreneurs. Moreover, utilizing a longitudinal study of 1053 ventures, Dahlqvist, Davidsson & Wiklund (2000) both demonstrated that founders' immigrant status had a negative effect on domestic new ventures' performance both in terms of marginal survival and high performance (sales growth, employment growth and profitability).

Therefore, in line with the current literature, I argue that in high growth industries such as high technology industries where access to resources and legitimacy in the mainstream economy is crucial for success; domestic-only new ventures with outsider founders will face greater hardships including costs similar to liabilities of foreignness, and will consequently have lower performance in terms of both survival and growth compared to domestic-only new ventures with insider founders.

However, I argue the reverse case when new ventures pursue early internationalization strategy. Although entering new markets involves considerable uncertainty and risk, entrepreneurs differ in their perceptions and in their capacities to manage them. Outsider entrepreneurs may handle this uncertainty and complexity of new foreign markets better due to their experiential knowledge and understanding of setting up and running businesses in their country of adoption. In particular, their exposure to customers, suppliers, competitors, regulators, and business professionals in their country of adoption is likely to provide outsider entrepreneurs with a capacity to deal with the challenges of new foreign markets.

Because outsider entrepreneurs learn, or develop a capacity to manage risk and deal with something "foreign" through their experiences in their country of adoption, this tacit knowledge of how to organize and manage international business is likely to be imprinted in the newly developing routines of immigrant-founded new ventures. Because firm behavior is largely routine-based and path-dependent, these operating routines developed in the country of adoption will help outsider founded new ventures manage the challenges of new foreign markets (Eriksson, Johanson, Majkgard & Sharma, 1997).

Insider entrepreneurs, on the other hand, start to operate their business in their native countries. Although they might try to gain some knowledge about operating internationally through external sources such as reports, documents, or the stories of other entrepreneurs,

Early Internationalization

because of the lack of tacit understanding and routines about managing international efforts, insider-founded new ventures are at disadvantage relative to outsider founded new ventures who possess greater knowledge of the pressures and challenges of foreign markets through their first hand experiences. If this line of reasoning is true, then outsider -founded international new ventures would better handle the risks of the new markets and have higher probability of survival and a greater degree of growth compared to insider-founded international new ventures. The above arguments lead to following two hypotheses on the interaction effect between founders' immigrant status and early internationalization strategy on firm survival and growth:

H3a: The effect of founders ' immigrant status on firm survival depends on whether the venture is early internationalized or not such that when the venture is domestic- only, founders' immigrant status is negatively related to firm survival. When the venture is early internationalized, founders' immigrant status is positively related to firm survival.

H3b: The effect of founders ' immigrant status on firm growth depends on whether the venture is early internationalized or not such that when the venture is domestic-only, founders' immigrant status is negatively related to firm growth. When the venture is early internationalized, founders' immigrant status is positively related to firm growth.

Summary
The relationships are shown in Figure 1. I investigate the role of founders' outsider status in explaining firm international strategy and performance. The objective is to understand (1) how *"outsiderness"* (and insiderness) affects entrepreneurs' decisions to internationalize early, and (2) how outsiderness affects new venture performance. Specifically, by drawing on the behavioral theory of the firm, I have argued that founders' outsider status encourages internationalization efforts by contributing entrepreneurs' global mindsets and eliminating

some of the cognitive and relational barriers to early internationalization that are common to insider entrepreneurs. Moreover, I have argued that outsiderness is not an inherent advantage or disadvantage, but its effect on firm performance is contingent on firm strategy (i.e. whether the firm is international or domestic-only). In particular, I have argued that for new ventures that follow a domestic strategy, outsiderness might be a disadvantage while it might be an advantage for new ventures that follow an international strategy. If the model I propose is indeed the case, then we can better understand why new ventures cross borders when they are so young, and we can also conclude that the focus on the disadvantages of outsiderness in the literature might be the result of ignoring new ventures' international strategies.

Figure 1: Theoretical Model

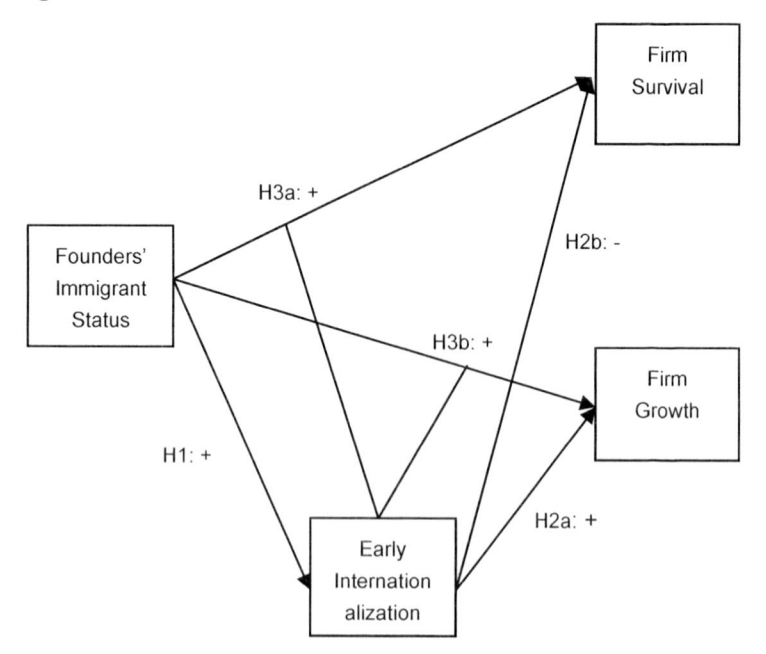

CHAPTER 5
The Context of the Study

High technology new ventures in the U.S. are selected as the context of this study. High technology ventures are chosen because it is an empirical setting that provides sufficient variation in the market scope of new ventures (i.e. domestic-only versus international) and founders' immigrant status (i.e. immigrant versus native). First, research demonstrates that early internationalization is more prevalent in high technology industries characterized by high degree of global integration, faster technological change, intense domestic competition, and high rates of industry growth. In fact, some scholars even argue that internationalization is a phenomenon specific to new ventures in high technology industries (e.g., Anderson, Gabrielsson & Wictor, 2004). Second, a growing body of research documents the increasing prevalence of immigrant entrepreneurs in the high technology industries in the U.S. Statistics show that 25% of all high-tech startups started in the U.S. in the last fifteen years had at least one immigrant entrepreneur in the founding team (Wadhwa et al., 2007). The majority of these highly skilled immigrants come to US for higher education. Many of them earn masters and PhD degrees in science and technology fields from US universities, and work for US corporations before they start their own businesses (Economist, March 2009).

Moreover, choosing the United States as home country base of these ventures has an advantage in that early internationalization strategy in the U.S. is more a preference than a forced choice because the size of the market is large enough to be self-sufficient (Etemad, 2004). Therefore, the variation in strategy leads itself to be explained by firm level characteristics rather than country level push factors. Finally, high technology industries are inherently important contexts to study firm strategy and performance. These sectors contribute to innovation, job creation, and productivity growth at significantly higher rates than do other sectors. Also, given that the impact of new ventures on innovation, job creation, and market competition are greater than that of large established firms in high technology industries (Kirchhoff & Spencer, 2007), the economic impact of these young companies makes them worthy of special scholarly attention.

Sample Data Collection

Firm level data to test the hypotheses come from a secondary data source – the Kaufmann Firm Survey (KFS), which is a large panel data set of new businesses founded in 2004. This data set is the largest and most recent longitudinal dataset of young ventures currently available. The data set consists of four follow up surveys (of the same firms) taking place in 2005, 2006, 2007, and 2008 respectively. The primary owner of each firm is contacted via online surveys and telephone survey programs for responses to detailed questions on business characteristics, business strategy and innovation, business structure and benefits, financing, and the demographic characteristics of the founders (DesRoches, Robb & Mulcahy, 2010).

The target population for the KFS is all the new businesses that were started in the 2004 calendar year in the United States. This population excludes any branch or subsidiary owned by an existing business, a business inherited from someone else, and non-profit startups. To be classified as a new business in the KFS, at least one of the following activities must have been conducted for the first time in the reference year (2004): payment of state unemployment (UI) taxes; payment of Federal Insurance Contributions Act (FICA) taxes; presence of legal status for the business; use of an Employer Identification Number (EIN); or use of a Schedule C tax form to report business income on a personal tax return.

The firms analyzed herein come from the Dun & Bradstreet (D&B) list of randomly chosen new businesses that started in 2004. In this data set, high-tech firms are intentionally oversampled by the Kaufmann Foundation. High technology firms are defined based on the categorization by Hadlock, Hecker & Gannon (1991). This definition considers the industry percentage of R&D employment and classifies the businesses into technology groups based on their Standard Industrialization Classification (SIC). The firms classified in the high-technology strata have the following two digits SIC codes: 28: Chemicals and allied products, 35: Industrial machinery and equipments, 36: Electrical and electronic equipment and 38: Instruments and related products.

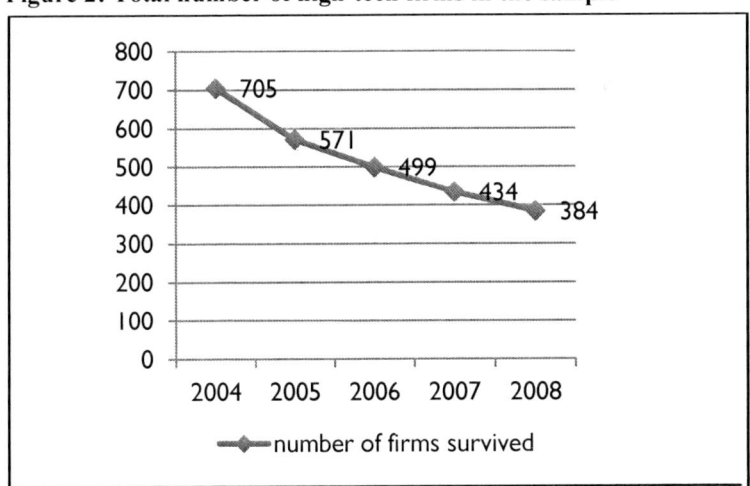

Figure 2: Total number of high-tech firms in the sample

[Line chart showing number of firms surviving: 2004: 705, 2005: 571, 2006: 499, 2007: 434, 2008: 384]

The sample for the first follow up survey, which was conducted between July 2005 and July 2006 includes 705 high-technology firms that agreed to participate in the study in the baseline survey in 2004. The response rate for the first follow up survey was 86 %, meaning that 571 firms completed the survey questions. The second follow up survey, conducted between May 2007 and December 2007, includes 499 firms, because of the original 705 firms, 93 were identified as out of business and 113 refused to participate in the second follow up survey. The third follow up survey was conducted between June 2008 and December 2008, and it includes 434 eligible firms remaining in the KSF panel, with 52 cases going out of business, and 126 refusing to participate. Finally, the fourth follow up survey, conducted between January 2009 and June 2009, includes 384 firms, with 57 going out of business and 119 not responding. Figure 2 shows the number of high technology businesses in the final sample by year.

The survey provides detailed information on owner characteristics. The data includes the immigrant status of the founders, their age, gender, race, education, previous industry experience and start up experience, providing a more comprehensive picture of founders. Moreover, the dataset includes detailed financial performance indicators, including firm survival, sales growth, profitability, ROA, and ROE.

Because immigrant status is time invariant, panel models are not appropriate to test my hypotheses. Therefore, I constructed a cross sectional data set by taking 2007 (year 3) as the base year at which I measured early internationalization. I measured the control variables in the same year. In alternative analyses, I lagged them one year and measured them, in year 2006[3]. Finally, I measured firm survival and growth one year following the base year, in year 2008. Table 1 shows the number of immigrant-founded and native-founded international and domestic-only ventures in the sample in the base year 3 (2007).

Table 1: Number of firms in 2007 (year 3)

	Domestic-only	Early Internationalized	Total
Native-founded	238	112	350
Immigrant-founded	23	22	45
Total	261	134	395

---

[3] Results are robust to these alternative specifications

The Context of the Study

Dependent Variables
The dependent variables that are employed in this study are: 1) Early internationalization, 2) Firm survival, 3) Firm growth.

Early Internationalization:
Early internationalization is a dummy variable to the following question asked in year 3 (2007): *"In 2007, were any of your company's sales made to individuals, businesses, or governments outside the US?"* No=0, and Yes=1. Firms that answered "yes" to this question are considered as early internationalizers because they crossed borders within the first three years of their existence, a categorization consistent with prior literature (Knight & Cavusgil, 2004; Zahra & George, 2002).

Firm Survival:
Firm survival is measured as a dummy variable to the following questions: *"Did your company permanently close operations"?* Yes=1, No=0 (reverse coded to indicate firm survival). The data included firm exits due to mergers or acquisitions. However, I have not considered them as firm failure because although mergers measure the discontinuity of the firm, only closing permanently captures permanent exit, which is more likely to be due to underperformance. This conceptualization and measurement is also consistent with extant research on firm failure (Thornhill & Amit, 2003).

I have chosen firm survival as one of the main performance indicators for the following reasons. First, for new firms it usually takes some time to achieve profitability and other dimensions of performance. Second, given approximately 50% of new ventures fail within 5 years, survival for a new venture is a critical performance achievement (Shane, 2007). Finally, due to lack of data, past studies suffer from survivor bias where only successful firms (not failed ones) are included in the sample for empirical analysis (Keupp & Gassmann, 2009). I use firm survival as a performance measure to overcome this methodological limitation of prior studies.

Firm Growth:
I constructed firm growth as the sales growth of sales in the year following early internationalization. This variable is computed as

follows: Sales Growth $_{2008}$ = (Sales Volume $_{2008}$ − Sales Volume $_{2007}$) / Sales Volume $_{2007}$. This operationalization is also consistent with the current literature (e.g. Fernhaber & Li, 2010). I chose sales growth as a performance indicator because sales growth is necessary for new ventures to fund future operations and to ensure their long-term survival (Robinson, 1999).

I chose to measure sales growth instead of profits because for new ventures that are in need of investing large sums of money into the business initially, they often don't start to make profits quickly. It takes some time to pay out the initial costs and become profitable. Therefore, measuring profits when the venture is very young (such as those new ventures in my sample) may not reflect the true potential of a new venture. On the other hand, sales growth from one year to the next might indicate the increasing customer acceptance of a new venture's products/services, and might better reflect a new venture's true long-term potential.

Independent Variables
This section explains how founders' immigrant status and control variables are determined and measured.

Founders' Immigrant Status:
Immigrant status is measured as a dummy variable to the following question in year 3 (2007): *Were you born in the U.S.?* Yes=1, No=0. This definition of immigrant as a non-U.S born person is also consistent with the prior literature (e.g. Hart, Acs & Tracy, 2009; Wadhwa et al., 2007). A primary founder, who was not born in the U.S. is classified as an immigrant and coded as "1" (and "0" otherwise). For new ventures with more than one founder, the primary founder is defined as the founder who has the largest equity share of the company. If founders have equal equity shares, then primary owner is designated as the one who is more involved with the day to day operations. In the final sample, 56% of the new ventures have one founder, while 30% have two founders, 10% have three founders and 4% have four or more founders. Moreover, in the final sample, 12% of the firms have an immigrant entrepreneur as the primary founder.

Table 2: Variable Definitions

VARIABLE	ABBREVATION of VARIABLES	DEFINITION
Firm Survival	Survival	Dummy =0 if firm is out of business, 0 otherwise
Firm Growth	Growth	Sales Volume $_{2008}$ − Sales Volume $_{2007}$) / Sales Volume$_{2007}$
Likelihood of Early Internationalization	Early International	Dummy =1 if firm has international sales, 0 otherwise
Domestic Geographic Market Scope	Domestic Scope	1= In neighborhoods local to business & In the same city or county, 2= In the same state, 3= Nationwide
Founders' Immigrant Status	Immigrant Status	Dummy ==1 if non-US born, 0 otherwise
Gender of the Primary Founder	Gender	Dummy =1 if founder is male, 0 otherwise
Age of the Primary Founder	Age	Age of the founder
Education of the Primary Founder	Education	1=High school or less, 2=Technical/Trade/Vocational degree, 3= Some collage, no degree, 4= Associate's degree, 5= Bachelor's Degree, 6= Some graduate school, no degree, 7= Master's degree, 8= Professional School, Doctorate.
Previous Industry Experience of the Primary Founder	Industry Exp	Years of experience that the founder have had in the industry in which the firm competes
Previous Startup Experience of the Primary Founder	Startup Exp	Number of other businesses started by the founder
Product or Service Company	Providing Product	Dummy 1= if firm provides product, 0 otherwise

Table 2: Variable Definitions (Continued)

VARIABLE	ABBREVATION of VARIABLES	DEFINITION
Internet Sales	Internet Sales	Dummy 1= if firm has internet sales, 0 otherwise
Intellectual Property	Intellectual Property	Dummy=1 if firm has either patents, copyrights or trademarks, 0 otherwise
R&D Focus	R&D Focus	Number of employees in R&D/Total number of employees
Sales Focus	Sales Focus	Number of employees in sales/Total number of employees
Firm Size	Total Assets	Total Assets (log)
The Mobility of Firm Resource Configuration	Resource Mobility	Liquid assets ($) / Total assets ($) Liquid assets: cash + account receivable + inventory
Past Firm Performance	ROA	Return on Asset (ROA): $Profit / $ Total Assets
VC Funding	VC Funding	Dummy=1 if firm is VC funded, 0 otherwise
Technology Generating Industry	Technology Generating	Dummy=1 if firm is operating in a technology generating industry, 0 otherwise
High-Tech Center	High-Tech Center	Dummy=1 if firm is located in a high-tech center at the zip code level, 0 otherwise
State Export Intensity	State Export Intensity	The number of exporters in a state /Total number of exporters in the U.S.

Some studies use the mere existence of an immigrant in the founding team to classify the new venture as an immigrant versus a native-founded company (e.g. Chaganti, Watts, Chaganti & Zimmerman-Treichel, 2008). While founders are the most influential people in new ventures, and this classification might have some value, because not all founders might be equally active or influential in directing the venture, by taking a more conservative approach, I choose to use the existence of immigrants as the "primary founder" to classify the new venture as an immigrant- versus a native-founded.

Control Variables
In order to minimize omitted variable bias, several individual, firm level and macro level control variables are used. These variables are presented below.

Individual Level Controls:
Gender. Prior research shows that female owned businesses take less risk and therefore, they may be less likely to internationalize, or serve broader markets (Reavley et. al, 2005), and that they tend to perform worse relative to male owned businesses (Orser, Riding, & Townsend, 2004).

Age. Although the influence of an entrepreneur's age on new venture strategies and performance is not well-established in the literature, it is an important variable to control. The reason for this is that age is likely correlated with the amount of time that entrepreneurs have spent in the US, causing variation in entrepreneurs' embeddedness in the US, which in turn may affect the propensity of firms to internationalize (Bonte, Falck & Heblich, 2009).

Education. Prior studies have observed a positive effect of education level of entrepreneurs on internationalization and geographic market scope (Nummela, Saarenketo & Puumalaonen, 2004), and has a concave relationship with new venture performance (Shane, 2007).

Previous start up Experience. Previous start up experience positively influences firm strategy and performance as entrepreneurs learn not only from their past mistakes but also from their confidence in formulating and implementing strategies (Shane, 2007).

Previous industry experience. Previous industry experience positively influences firm strategy and performance as entrepreneurs gain expertise about their industry, develop social networks, and get deeper understanding about their customers through their industry experiences (Dencker, Gruber & Shah, 2009).

Firm Level Controls:
Main industrial activity (Providing product or service). Prior research shows that manufacturing firms are more likely to enter international markets early relative to service firms (Westhead et. al, 1995).
Internet sales. Prior research argues that internet is a tool that facilitates early internationalization by making it much easier to reach customers all over the world. In fact, the existing literature asserts that the internet is one of the most important technological developments giving rise to early internationalization (Madsen & Servais, 1997).
Intellectual property. Studies show that innovation is positively related to internationalization and performance of new ventures because innovative products or services do not demand low cost strategy and/or scale economies to successfully enter and operate in international markets, and facilitates new venture internationalization (Andersson et al., 2004).
R&D focus. Prior studies show that R&D intensity, or how much a firm spends on R&D as a percentage of total sales, positively affects its internationalization because in the long run R&D spending results either in product or process innovations, making the firm more competitive to operate in international markets (Salomon & Shaver, 2005). Although this measure is a common measure in the IB field, in this study I use R&D focus, or the number of R&D employees as a percentage of total number employees. New ventures are often in need of getting financial resources and establishing themselves in the market place. In this process, their R&D spending and total sales show very large fluctuations independent of the true effort put into the R&D. Therefore, I use R&D focus instead of R&D intensity in order to get at the real R&D focus of the firm. This measure is also used in the extant literature in international entrepreneurship (e.g. Jones, 1999)
Sales focus. Prior studies show that how much a firm spends on advertising and promotion as a percentage of total sales positively affects its internationalization. These investments help attract customers making the firm more competitive in international markets (Salomon & Shaver, 2005). I use sales focus the number of sales employees as a percentage of total number employees instead of sales spending. The reason is that being young and resource constrained, new ventures cannot often afford a lot of resources to promotion related

activities, and their sales very largely fluctuate. Therefore, I use sales focus instead of sales intensity in order to get at the real effort that the new venture put into the sales and promotion activities.

Firm Size. Firm size has consistently been shown as a factor facilitating internationalization of new ventures (Andersen et. al., 2004; Westhead, Wright & Ucbasaran, 2001). Because internationalization is costly and requires additional resources, larger firms are more likely to survive these costs. I measure firm size in two ways. One is the log of total assets ($) value and the second is the log of total number of employees. These operationalizations are also consistent with the extant literature (e.g. Schwens & Kabst, 2009b; Jones, 1999).

The Mobility of firm resources. Mobility of firm resource configuration is measured as a continuous variable. It is computed as the dollar value of liquid assets over the dollar value of total assets (liquid assets ($) / total assets ($)). This conceptualization of asset mobility is also consistent with literature on corporate finance that asserts that liquid assets are more readily allocated for alternative investments than fixed assets (Fazzari, Hubbard & Petersen, 1988).

Prior Performance. Studies show that prior performance of new ventures affect future strategies and actions (Bromiley, 2005). There are many prior performance measures such ROA, ROE, profit margin name to name a few. In this study, I use return on assets (ROA) as a performance measure because ROA avoids distortions due to differences in financial leverage across firms. To control for a behavioral implication of performance on subsequent strategy, this variable is lagged one year.

VC Funding. Research suggests VCs have a positive effect on survival by providing new ventures with financial, managerial, and reputational resources (Shane 2002). In addition to the effect of VC financing on firm strategy and performance, the research also shows that VC firms tend to invest in more promising or better quality ventures in the market place (Bhide, 2008). In that sense, it is important to control for VC financing to capture both *a priori* quality of the venture as well as the additional effect of VCs, both of which might have implications for firm strategy and performance. I measure VC financing as a dummy variable, which takes a value of 1 if the new venture has VC financing, 0 otherwise.

Macro Controls:
Technology Generator Industry[4]. Prior research shows that industry characteristics, -particularly R&D activities - have important effects on new venture internationalization and performance (Shrader, Oviatt & McDougall (2000). Industries differ in their innovativeness even within high technology industries. This variable is constructed such that if a new venture operates in an industry that has above average R&D spending or R&D employment, it is coded as 1, 0 otherwise.

High-tech Center. Prior research shows that locating in high-tech centers provide firms with access to resources and knowledge through agglomeration economies and enhances firm performance (Chung & Alcácer, 2010). I measure this variable as a dummy variable such that if a new venture and a high-tech center are located in an area under the same 2 digit zip code, then I assigned a value of 1 to that new venture and 0 otherwise. There are twenty-two high-tech centers in fourteen different states in the U.S.[5]. I have utilized U.S. States Postal Service website[6] to identify and match the zip codes of high-tech centers with the zip codes of new ventures in my sample.

State Export Intensity. Research shows that firms follow strategies due to institutional pressures, also called isomorphism. For example, Fernhaber & Li (2010) examines 150 U.S. based new ventures and shows that new venture international entry was an imitative response to the internationalization of other firms. Thus, I control for the export intensity of the state in which a new venture is located. I measure this variable as the number of exporters in a state divided by the total number of exporters in the U.S. I get this information from U.S. Census Bureau Statistics (2010).

---

[4] I have also controlled for 2-digit SIC codes by creating 4 dummy variables for each of the following industries within the high technology strata. These industries are: Chemicals and allied products, Industrial machinery and equipment, electrical and electronic equipment and Instruments and related products. However, because none of these dummy variables were significant in any of the analyses, the final results presented here do not include industry dummies.

[5] See Appendix A for the complete list of the high-tech centers in the United States.

[6] http://zip4.usps.com/zip4/citytown.jsp

CHAPTER 6
Outsider Entrepreneurs: More International but not More Successful

Table 3[7] reports descriptive statistics and Table 4 presents pair-wise correlations for some selected variables used in the analyses. Pair-wise correlations among the variables are generally as expected. The values in Table 4 indicate that *early internationalization* is positively and significantly (as expected) related to *founder immigrant status*. Consistent with prior literature, *male* and *education* on the individual level are significantly and positively correlated with *early internationalization*. Moreover, *intellectual property*, and *state export intensity* at the firm and context level are significantly and positively correlated with *early internationalization*. Table 4 suggests that *immigrant* entrepreneurs tend to be more *educated*, tend to locate in *high-tech centers* and in states with high *state export intensity*. This is as expected.

---

[7] The best way to ensure the accuracy of the data is to proof read the original data. However, since the data comes from a secondary source, descriptive statistics are used to evaluate the data accuracy and identify the problematic cases for the variables. Table 3 shows no out of range case, or a variable with strange mean, median or standard deviation values.

Table 3: Descriptive Statistics

VARIABLE	N	Mean	Median	Std. Dev
Dependent Variables				
Sales Growth	391	0.61	0	3.67
Survival	393	0.91	1	0.28
Early International	405	0.34	0	0.48
Immigrant Status	434	0.11	0	0.31
Male	434	0.83	1	0.37
Age	429	47.34	47	10.26
Education	432	6.47	7	2.09
Prev. Industry Experience	433	14.85	15	11.45
Prev. Startup Experience	431	1.20	1	2.08
Providing Product	434	0.75	1	0.43
Internet Sales	402	0.29	0	0.46
Intellectual Property	433	0.33	0	0.47
R&D Focus	334	0.37	0.16	0.56
Sales Focus	334	0.53	0.69	0.35
Resource Mobility	414	0.61	0.69	0.35
Total Assets ($)	434	$665,117	$114,500	$1,851,459
VC Funded	310	0.04	0	0.20
ROA	373	-0.15	0.03	2.72
Tech Generating Industry	434	0.16	0	0.37
High-Tech Center	423	0.37	0	0.48
State Export Int.	434	4.5	2.6	4.35

Table 4: Pairwise Correlations

	Variables	1	2	3	4	5	6	7	8	9	10
1	Sales Growth	1									
2	Survival	.00	1								
3	Early Int.	.03	.05	1							
4	Immigrant Status	.06	-.06	.13*	1						
5	Male	.04	.02	.10*	.04	1					
6	Education	.04	.12*	.24*	.21*	.06	1				
7	Intellectual Property	.11*	-.02	.19*	.07	-.06	.41*	1			
8	VC Funded	.07	.01	.11	.10	.12*	.14*	.11	1		
9	High-Tech Center	-.07	.06	.06	.10*	.00	.12*	.04	.03	1	
10	State Export Intensity	.03	.02	.10*	.15*	-.06	.04	.00	-.04	.33*	1

Table 5 presents t-tests for immigrant and native-founded new ventures on some of the key variables. Immigrant-founded new ventures internationalize earlier and have more mobile resources than native-founded new ventures, both of which is expected due to the limited embeddedness of immigrant founders in their adopted countries. Moreover, immigrant-founders are more educated, are more likely to get VC financing, and are more likely to have more intellectual property relative to native founders and these differences are significant for education and VC financing respectively. This reflects that immigrant-founded new ventures are more innovative and they are rewarded by the private equity market for that. This seems to show that immigrant-founded new ventures are not being discriminated in the VC market although there is empirical evidence for their limited access to bank financing (Bates, 1997). Moreover, although native-founded new ventures have larger total assets, this difference is not significant.

Table 5: Comparison of the Means of Key Variables for Immigrant vs. Native-Founded New Ventures

VARIABLE	Immigrant-Founded	Native-Founded	t-statistics	p-value
Sales Growth	0.693 (0.488)	0.358 (0.115)	-1.064	0.367
Survival	0.902 (0.046)	0.914 (0.015)	0.26	0.793
Early International	0.511 (0.075)	0.319 (0.024)	-2.59	0.010*
Education	7.602 (0.233)	6.308 (0.082)	-5.54	0.000**
Intellectual Property	0.420 (0.071)	0.322 (0.024)	-1.38	0.168
VC Funded	0.150 (0.057)	0.065 (0.013)	-1.94	0.053**
Resource Mobility	0.709 (0.044)	0.603 (0.018)	-1.94	0.053**
Total Assets ($)	246,556 (95,789)	434,794 (62,804)	1.11	0.268
High-Tech Center	0.500 (0.073)	0.355 (0.024)	-1.97	0.049**
State Export Intensity	6.136 (0.687)	4.280 (0.216)	-3.086	0.002**

*p <0.10, **p<0.05 (standard deviations are in parentheses), two-tailed test.

Moreover, new ventures with immigrant founders are more likely to be located in high-tech centers and in states with higher export intensity. This again might be the result of the greater flexibility that immigrant-founded new ventures have relative to native-founded new ventures in their location choice due to their limited embeddedness in their adopted country. Finally, as expected, there is no difference between immigrant and native-founded new ventures in terms of their performance in sales growth or survival rates. It is also important to note that the variance within the immigrant group is larger than the variance within the native group for each of the variables.

Table 6: Comparison of the Means of Key Variables for Domestic-Only vs. International New Ventures

VARIABLE	International	Domestic Only	t-statistics	p-value
Sales Growth	0.434 (0.183)	0.374 (0.147)	-0.25	0.806
Survival	0.934 (0.022)	0.902 (0.019)	-1.01	0.312
Immigrant Status	0.164 (0.031)	0.080 (0.017)	-2.59	0.010*
Education	7.065 (0.165)	6.014 (0.125)	-4.98	0.000**
Intellectual Property	0.435 (0.042)	0.243 (0.026)	-4.065	0.000**
VC Funded	0.063 (0.023)	0.022 (0.011)	-1.805	0.072*
Resource Mobility	0.736 (0.025)	0.553 (0.022)	-5.179	0.000**
Total Assets ($)	811,718 (137,332)	479,798 (94,267)	-2.02	0.044**
High-Tech Center	0.406 (0.042)	0.347 (0.029)	-1.14	0.254
State Export Intensity	5.071 (0.389)	4.156 (0.251)	-2.05	0.042**

*p <0.10, **p<0.05 (standard deviations are in parentheses). two-tailed test.

Table 6 presents t-tests for domestic-only and international new ventures on some of the key variables. As expected, the founders of international new ventures are more likely to be immigrants and have more education relative to the founders of domestic-only new ventures. These differences are significant. Moreover, international new ventures are significantly more likely to have intellectual property, more mobile resources, more assets, and they are more likely to get VC financing relative to domestic-only new ventures. These significant differences echo the idea in the current literature that international new ventures tend to be rich technologically cutting-edge and agile companies. International new ventures are also significantly more likely to be located in states with greater export intensity relative to domestic-only new ventures. Surprisingly however, in the t-test analysis, no significant difference is observed between international and domestic-only new ventures in terms of both survival and growth. Finally, the variance within the international group is larger than the variance within the domestic-only group for each of the variables.

Results on Early Internationalization

Table 7 presents the results from estimates of logistic regressions. The dependent variable is early internationalization. The dependent variable in the model is a dummy variable measuring whether a new venture has any international sales. To test Hypothesis 1, whether founders' immigrant status encourages new ventures to be early internationalizers, *immigrant status* has a positive and significant effect on the *likelihood of early internationalization* with z = 1.68, p<0.10, proving support for the H1. The odds ratio implies that new ventures with immigrant founders are 2.37 times are more likely to be early internationalizers relative to new ventures with native founders.

Moreover, the first column in Table 7 shows that founders' *education* is positive and significant, indicating that the more educated the founder is, the more likely that his/her venture is an early internationalizer. Moreover, consistent with current literature, *Providing Product, Internet sales, Resource Mobility, Total Assets, VC Funding and Past Performance* are all positive and significant indicating that those larger, VC-funded product new ventures with more mobile resources and internet sales are more likely to internationalize early. Moreover, new ventures that operate in technology generating industries are less likely to be early international than those that do not operate in technology generating industries.

Results on Firm Survival

Table 8 presents the results from the estimates of ivprobit regression testing Hypothesis 2a, whether early internationalization affects new venture survival. The dependent variable in the regression is firm survival, measuring whether a new venture is out of business in the year following early internationalization.

Table 7: Test of H1: Logistic Estimate of the Likelihood of Early Internationalization

Estimators→ Variables ↓	Odds Ratio	St. Error	z	p>|z|
Immigrant Status	**2.37**	**0.515**	**1.68**	**0.094**
Male	0.98	0.554	-0.04	0.966
Age	0.99	0.016	-0.70	0.486
Education	1.21*	0.092	2.07	0.038
Prev. Industry Experience	1.03	0.019	1.49	0.137
Prev. Startup Experience	1.08	0.099	0.77	0.442
Providing Product	2.91**	0.430	2.48	0.013
Internet Sales	2.68**	0.384	2.57	0.010
Intellectual Property	1.39	0.379	0.86	0.389
R&D Focus	0.45	0.567	-1.42	0.155
Sales Focus	0.51	0.673	-1.01	0.312
Resource Mobility	2.85*	0.608	1.72	0.085
Log(Total Assets $)	1.26**	0.113	2.04	0.041
VC Funded	9.50**	1.079	2.09	0.037
Past Performance (ROA_2)	1.39***	0.127	2.60	0.009
Tech Generator Industry	0.28***	0.440	-2.93	0.003
High -Tech Center	1.50	0.381	1.05	0.292
State Export Intensity	1.05	0.042	1.04	0.297
Log Likelihood	-111.812			
N	215			

Note. *p<0.10; **p<0.05; ***<0.01

I estimate a two stage ivprobit regression to address the endogeneity problem, which is caused by omitted variable(s) that affect(s) both early internationalization and firm survival simultaneously. This estimation is a two stage model where a probit regression is first used to estimate the independent variable by using an instrumental variable in the first stage, and the predicted values from this regression equation are calculated and used in the second stage to predict the dependent variable. However, instead of constructing two stage estimates, I use STATA to do the estimation by using the ivprobit command. This eliminates the problem of getting incorrect standard errors.

This technique is viable only when that there exists an instrumental variable that has the property that changes in this variable are associated with changes in the independent variable but do not lead to change in dependent variable apart from the indirect route via the independent variable, also called the "exclusion restriction" (Angrist & Pishke, 2009). Specifically, instrumental variables should satisfy the following two conditions. 1) The instrument must be correlated with the endogenous explanatory variable, conditional on the other covariates. 2) The instrument cannot be correlated with the error term in the explanatory equation, that is, the instrument cannot suffer from the same problem as the original predicting variable.

In order to find a good instrument, it is important to have a good institutional knowledge of the research context and especially of the processes determining the independent variable. I choose "main industrial activity" as an instrumental variable to get the predicted values of early internationalization in the first stage because while there are theoretical reasons and empirical evidence that main industrial activity may affect early internationalization (i.e.; product firms are more likely to be international than service firms, Westhead, 1995), it is not very plausible that producing a product versus service would significantly affect firm survival or growth. As can be seen in the Table 8, the coefficient of *providing product* is significant with z = 3.67 at p<0.000 level. In the second stage, the predicted values of early internationalization from the first regression are used to predict firm survival.

Table 8 shows that the coefficient of the predicted values of early internationalization is negative and significant in predicting firm survival with z=-1.75 at p<0.0001 level, providing support for Hypothesis 2a. Table 8 also shows that coefficients for education and total assets are positive and significant, indicating that larger new ventures with more educated founders are more likely to survive than those smaller new ventures with less educated founders.

Table 8: Test of H2a: Instrumental Variable Probit (ivprobit) Estimation of Firm Survival

Estimators→ Variables ↓	β	St. Deviation	Z	p>|z|
Second Stage				
Early International (predicted values)	-1.754***	0.526	-3.33	0.001
Immigrant Status	0.055	0.304	0.18	0.857
Education	0.268***	0.084	3.18	0.001
Prev. Industry Experience	0.008	0.007	1.00	0.316
Prev. Startup Experience	-0.029	0.051	-0.56	0.574
Intellectual Property	0.024	0.256	0.10	0.924
Log(Total Assets $)	0.130***	0.042	3.12	0.002
Tech Generator Industry	-0.690**	0.280	-2.46	0.014
Past Performance (ROA)	0.017	0.026	0.67	0.502
High -Tech Center	0.239	0.197	1.21	0.266
Constant (α)	-1.489***	0.530	-2.81	0.005
First Stage (Predicting Early International)				
Immigrant Status	0.149*	0.077	1.93	0.053
Education	0.037**	0.013	2.91	0.004
Prev. Industry Experience	0.005**	0.002	2.44	0.015
Prev. Startup Experience	0.015	0.013	1.10	0.269
Intellectual Property	0.087	0.060	1.46	0.146
Log(Total Assets $)	0.035**	0.011	3.03	0.002
Tech Generator Industry	-0.102	0.065	-1.56	0.118
Past Performance (ROA_2)	0.006	0.009	0.61	0.541
High -Tech Center	0.038	0.050	0.76	0.446
Provide Product	0.189***	0.052	3.67	0.000
Constant (α)	-0.593***	0.136	-4.37	0.000
Athro	0.93	0.538	1.73	0.084
Lnsigma	-0.841	0.025	-32.74	0.000
Log Likelihood	-258.169			
N	331			

Table 9: Test of H2b: Instrumental Variable Regression (ivreg) Estimation Effect of Firm Growth

Estimators→ Variables ↓	β	St. Dev.	Z	p>|z|
Second Stage				
Early International (predicted values)	3.966	2.708	1.46	0.145
Immigrant Status	-1.401	1.197	-1.17	0.244
Male	0.522	0.773	0.67	0.500
Education	-0.151	0.207	-0.73	0.466
Prev. Industry Experience	-0.043	0.033	-1.30	0.194
Prev. Startup Experience	0.121	0.151	0.80	0.425
Internet Sales	-0.083	0.844	-0.10	0.921
Intellectual Property	1.008	0.962	1.05	0.296
Log(Total Assets_2 $)	0.621**	0.290	2.14	0.033
VC Funded	1.323	1.867	0.71	0.479
Tech Generator Industry	0.359	0.672	0.53	0.594
R&D Focus	0.559	1.530	0.37	0.715
Sales Focus	-0.950	1.055	-0.90	0.369
Log (Sales_2 $)	-1.801***	0.662	-2.72	0.007
High -Tech Center	-0.922	0.676	-1.36	0.174
Constant (α)	16.195**	6.199	2.61	0.010
First Stage (Predicting Early International)				
Immigrant Status	0.212*	0.111	1.91	0.058
Male	0.057	0.093	0.61	0.543
Education	0.031*	0.017	1.85	0.066
Prev. Industry Experience	0.004	0.003	1.49	0.137
Prev. Startup Experience	0.001	0.017	0.10	0.919
Internet Sales	0.176**	0.070	2.53	0.012
Intellectual Property	0.054	0.072	0.75	0.455
Log(Total Assets_2 $)	0.012	0.023	0.53	0.594
VC Funded	0.206	0.177	1.16	0.248
Tech Generator Industry	-0.204**	0.079	-2.60	0.010
R&D Focus	-0.116	0.079	-1.46	0.147

Table 9: Test of H2b: Instrumental Variable Regression (ivreg) Estimation Effect of Firm Growth (Continued)

Estimators→ Variables ↓	β	St. Dev.	Z	p>|z|
Sales Focus	-0.007	0.072	-0.11	0.913
Log (Sales_2 $)	0.035	0.031	1.15	0.250
High-Tech Center	0.115*	0.065	1.80	0.074
Provide Product	0.208**	0.080	2.60	0.010
Constant (α)	-0.741**	0.358	-2.07	0.040
R2	0.06			
N	221			

Results on Firm Growth

Table 9 presents the results from the estimates of an instrumental variable regression. The dependent variable in the regression is firm growth, measuring the average sales growth in the year following early internationalization. To test Hypothesis 2b, whether early internationalization affects new venture growth, I run an ivreg regression to address the endogeneity problem, which is caused by omitted variable(s) that affect(s) both early internationalization and firm growth simultaneously. I used *main industrial activity* as an instrumental variable to predict early internationalization in the first stage. As can be seen in the Table 9, the coefficient of *providing product is* significant with z = 2.60 at the 1% level. In the second stage, the predicted values of early internationalization from the first regression are used to predict firm growth.

Table 9 shows that the coefficient of the predicted values of early internationalization is positive but non-significant in predicting firm growth with z= 1.46 at p=0.15, providing support for the direction of the relationship but not for the significance of the relationship for Hypothesis 2b. Table 9 also shows that the coefficient for total assets is positive and significant, indicating that new ventures with more assets have higher growth rates than new ventures with fewer assets.

Results on the Interaction Effect of Immigrant Status and Early Internationalization on Firm Survival

In order to test Hypothesis 3a, or the interaction effect between immigrant status and early internationalization on firm survival, an ivprobit regression with an interaction term is run as specified in the estimation models section above. However, the maximum likelihood estimate that ivprobit regression uses did not convergence. The reason for the non-convergence was that interaction term estimated the success and failures perfectly. Therefore, Table 10 presents the results from the estimates of simple probit regression although this regression analysis is subject to omitted variable bias. Further, I conduct subsample analyses on immigrant versus native-founded and international versus domestic-only new ventures to illustrate Hypothesis 3a.

The dependent variable in the probit regression in Table 10 is firm survival, a dummy variable, measuring whether the new venture is out of business or not in the year following when the early internationalization is measured.

To test Hypothesis 3a, whether there is a significant interaction effect of immigrant status and early internationalization on firm survival, I add the interaction of *immigrant status* and *early internationalization* to the regression equation. As can be seen in Table 10, there is a significant interaction effect of immigrant status and early internationalization on firm survival with z =-2.31, at the 5% level, proving support for Hypothesis 3a that the relationship between founders' immigrant status and firm survival depends on whether the new venture is domestic-only or international.

The results also show that larger new ventures with more educated founders have a higher probability of survival than smaller new ventures with less educated founders. Moreover, new ventures that operate in technology generating high-tech industries have a lower probability of survival than those that do not operate in technology generating high technology industries. In addition, founders' immigrant status and early internationalization has no significant main effect on firm survival.

Table 10: Test of H3a: Probit Estimate of Firm Survival

Estimators→ Variables ↓	β	St. Dev	z	p>|z|
Immigrant Status	0.403	0.526	0.77	0.443
Early Internationalization	0.086	0.278	0.31	0.757
Immigrant Status * Early International (interaction)	-1.663**	0.720	-2.31	0.021
Education	0.334***	0.075	4.42	0.000
Prev. Industry Experience	-0.003	0.010	-0.31	0.758
Prev. Startup Experience	-0.097*	0.053	-1.83	0.067
Intellectual Property	-0.358	0.291	-1.23	0.217
Log(Total Assets $)	0.111**	0.051	2.16	0.031
Tech Generator Industry	-0.842***	0.292	-2.89	0.004
Past Performance (ROA_3)	0.002	0.024	0.09	0.928
High-Tech Center	0.340	0.254	1.34	0.181
Constant (α)	-1.283*	0.678	-1.89	0.058
Log Likelihood	-65.48			
N	331			

To detail the interaction effect, I also made subsample comparisons (1) between international and domestic-only new ventures to see the strength of difference in the relationship between immigrant status and firm survival under these two strategies, and (1) between immigrant-founded and native-founded new ventures to see the strength of difference in the relationship between internationalization strategy and firm survival under these two founder types. The results of these analyses are presented in the Appendix B.

Results on the Effect of Immigrant Status on Firm Survival for International versus Domestic-Only New Ventures

First, examining only international new ventures, I find that (see Table B.1 in Appendix B) that *immigrant status* has a negative and significant effect on firm survival with z = -2.58, p<0.05, contradicting Hypothesis 3a. It means that immigrant status has a negative effect on firm survival for international new ventures. Second, examine only domestic-only new ventures, I find that (see Table B.2 in Appendix B) *immigrant status* has no significant effect on firm survival. It means that immigrant status has no effect on the survival of domestic-only new ventures. In order to test the significance of this difference, I calculated marginal fixed effects for immigrant status in each of the subsample (international and domestic-only new ventures). These values are presented in the last rows both in Table B.1 and Table B.2 in appendix B. I then conduct a two sample t-test to test if the marginal fixed effects of immigrant status on firm survival in the sample of international new ventures and domestic-only new ventures are significantly different from each other.

Figure 3: Moderating Effect of Early Internationalization Strategy on the Relationship between Founders' Immigrant Status and Firm Survival

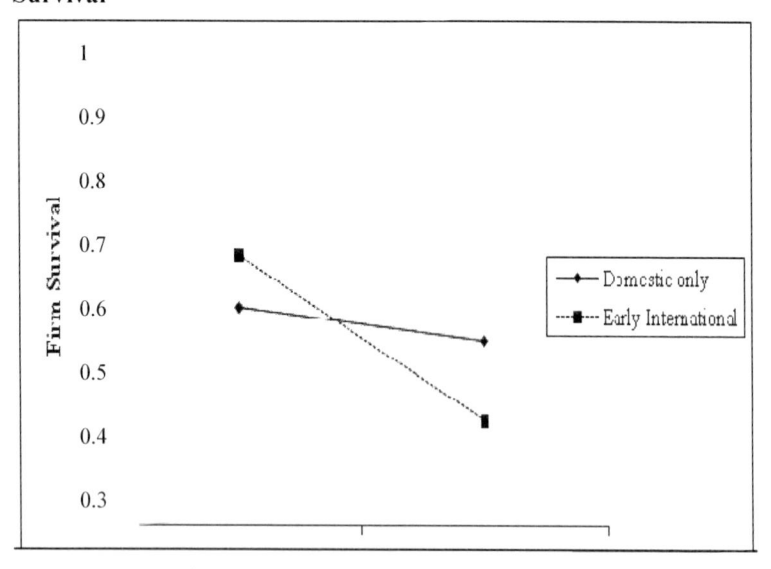

The result shows that the effect of immigrant status on firm survival is significantly different in the sample of international versus domestic-only new ventures with t=-1.878, $p<0.05$, providing statistical support for Hypothesis 3a although the effect is not in the direction that was hypothesized. Figure 3 presents the results graphically. It shows that for domestic-only new ventures, founders' immigrant status has no statistically significant effect on the probability of firm survival while for early internationalized new ventures, founders' immigrant status has a significant negative effect on the probability of firm survival.

Results on the Effect of Early Internationalization on Firm Survival for Immigrant versus Native-Founded New Ventures
First, examining solely immigrant-founded new ventures, I find that (See Table B.3 in Appendix B) *early internationalization* has a negative and significant effect on firm survival with $z = -2.31$, $p<0.05$, contradicting H3a. It means that early internationalization negatively affects the survival of immigrant-founded new ventures. Second, examining only native-founded new ventures, I find that (See Table B.4 in Appendix B) *early internationalization* has no significant effect on firm survival. It means that early internationalization strategy has no significant effect on the survival of native-founded new ventures.

In order to test the significance of this difference, I calculated marginal fixed effects for immigrant status in each of the subsample (immigrant and native-founded ventures). These values are presented in Table B.3 and Table B.4 in Appendix B. I then conduct a two sample t-test to test if the marginal fixed effects of early internationalization on firm survival in the sample of immigrant and native-founded new ventures are significantly different from each other.

The result shows that the effect of early internationalization on firm survival is not significantly different in the sample of immigrant versus native-founded new ventures. Figure 4 presents the results graphically. It shows that for native-founded new ventures; early internationalization has no statistically significant effect on the probability of firm survival while for immigrant-founded new ventures; early internationalization has a significant negative effect on the probability of firm survival but this difference is not statistically significant.

Figure 4: Moderating Effect of Founders' Immigrant Status on the Relationship between Early Internationalization Strategy and Firm Survival

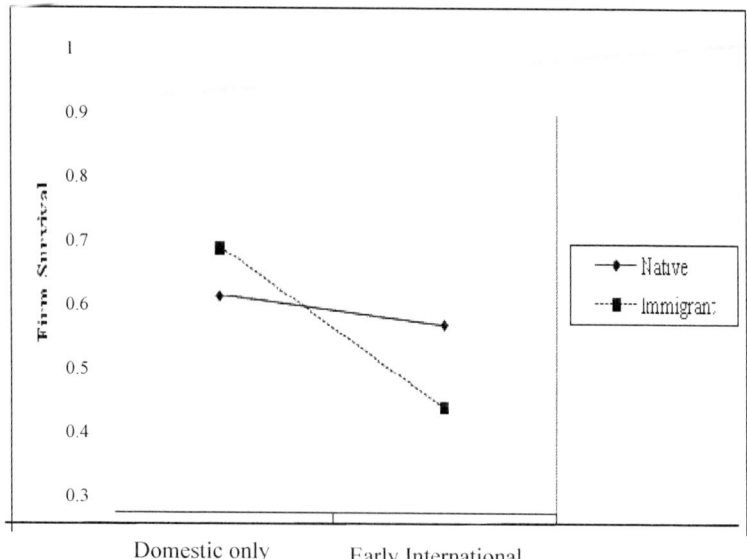

[Chart showing Firm Survival on y-axis (0.3 to 1) with two lines: Native (solid) declining slightly from ~0.65 to ~0.60, and Immigrant (dashed) declining steeply from ~0.75 to ~0.40, across x-axis categories "Domestic only" and "Early International"]

Results on the Interaction Effect of Immigrant Status and Early Internationalization on Firm Growth

Table 11 presents the results from instrumental variable regression analyses that tests Hypothesis 3b, the interaction effect between immigrant status and early internationalization on firm growth. I run an ivreg regression to address the endogeneity problem, which may be caused by omitted variable(s) that affect(s) both early internationalization and firm growth simultaneously. I used *main industrial activity* as an instrumental variable to predict early internationalization and the interaction of early internationalization and immigrant status in the first stage. Table 11 shows the results from ivreg analysis.

Table 11: Test of the Interaction Effect between Early Internationalization and Immigrant Status on Firm Growth

Estimators→ Variables ↓	β	St. Dev	Z	p>|z|
Second Stage				
Early Internationalization (predicted values)	4.368	3.077	1.42	0.157
Immigrant Status	-0.308	1.992	-0.15	0.877
Early International * Immigrant Status (predicted values)	**-1.992**	**4.702**	**-0.42**	**0.672**
Male	0.525	0.782	0.67	0.502
Education	-0.137	0.206	-0.66	0.508
Prev. Industry Experience	-0.045	0.034	1.32	0.189
Prev. Startup Experience	0.112	0.156	0.72	0.473
Internet Sales	-0.127	0.857	-0.15	0.883
Intellectual Property	0.941	0.963	0.98	0.330
Log(Total Assets_2 $)	0.626**	0.293	2.14	0.034
VC Funded	1.553	2.053	0.76	0.450
Tech Generator Industry	0.341	0.678	0.50	0.615
R&D Focus	0.521	1.554	0.34	0.738
Sales Focus	-0.937	1.056	-0.89	0.376
Log (Sales_2 $)	-1.819***	0.667	-2.73	0.007
High -Tech Center	-0.912	0.680	-1.34	0.181
Constant (α)	16.186	6.159	2.63	0.009
First Stage (Predicting Early International)				
Immigrant Status	0.159	0.202	0.79	0.432
Male	0.058	0.094	0.62	0.535
Education	0.031	0.017	1.82	0.070
Prev. Industry Experience	0.004	0.003	1.44	0.151
Prev. Startup Experience	0.002	0.017	0.10	0.924
Internet Sales	0.176**	0.070	2.51	0.013
Intellectual Property	0.056	0.073	0.77	0.441
Log(Total Assets_2 $)	0.012	0.022	0.53	0.597

Table 11: Test of the Interaction Effect between Early Internationalization and Immigrant Status on Firm Growth (Continued)

Estimators → Variables ↓	β	St. Dev	Z	p>|z|
VC Funded	0.196	0.181	1.08	0.279
Tech Generator Industry	-0.204**	0.080	-2.59	0.010
R&D Focus	-0.113	0.080	-1.41	0.159
Sales Focus	-0.009	0.073	-0.14	0.891
Log (Sales_2 $)	0.037	0.031	1.17	0.242
High -Tech Center	0.115*	0.065	1.77	0.078
Provide Product	0.199**	0.085	2.33	0.021
Immigrant * Provide Product	0.075	0.240	0.31	0.754
Constant (α)	-0.742**	0.359	-2.07	0.040
First Stage (Predicting Early International *Immigrant Status)				
Immigrant Status	0.327***	0.061	5.36	0.000
Male	0.019	0.028	0.68	0.494
Education	0.012**	0.005	2.35	0.020
Prev. Industry Experience	-0.001	0.001	-0.85	0.396
Prev. Startup Experience	-0.005	0.005	-0.91	0.363
Internet Sales	0.010	0.021	0.48	0.634
Intellectual Property	-0.013	0.022	-0.59	0.555
Log(Total Assets_2 $)	0.005	0.007	0.71	0.481
VC Funded	0.108**	0.054	1.98	0.049
Tech Generator Industry	-0.047	0.024	-1.99	0.048
R&D Focus	-0.029	0.024	-1.21	0.229
Sales Focus	-0.006	0.022	-0.25	0.799
Log (Sales_2 $)	0.002	0.009	0.29	0.771
High -Tech Center	0.022	0.020	1.12	0.263
Provide Product	-0.004	0.025	-0.14	0.886
Immigrant * Provide Product	0.375***	0.072	5.17	0.000
Constant (α)	-0.155	0.108	-1.43	0.155
R2	0.05			
N	221			

In the first stage, the coefficient of *providing product* is significant with z = 2.33 at p< 0.05 level in predicting early internationalization in the first stage. Similarly, results show that the coefficient of *providing product*immigrant status* is significant with z=5.17 p<0.000 in predicting the interaction term – *early internationalization*immigrant status* in the first stage. In the second stage, the predicted values of *early internationalization* and the predicted values of the interaction term - *early internationalization*immigrant status* from the first stage are used to predict firm growth in the second stage. Table 11 shows that the coefficient of the predicted values of the interaction term - *early internationalization*immigrant status* is not significant in the second stage, providing no support for H3b. Results also shows that the main effect of early internationalization and immigrant status are also non-significant. The only significant coefficients predicting firm growth in this regression analysis are firm size and prior sales.

Table 12 presents the estimates of OLS regression to check the consistency of the results across two estimation techniques. The dependent variable in the regression is firm growth, measuring the average sales growth in the year following early internationalization. To test whether there is a significant interaction effect of immigrant status and early internationalization on firm growth, I run a regression by adding the interaction of immigrant status and early internationalization to the regression equation. As can be seen in Table 12, while there is no significant main effect of immigrant status or early internationalization on sales growth, there is a significant interaction effect of immigrant status and early internationalization on sales growth with z = -2.32, p<0.05, proving support for the Hypothesis H3b.

Because OLS regression and ivreg regression analyses produces inconsistent results, which might be due to weakness of the instrumental variable, subsample analyses are conducted. I undertake subsample comparisons (1) between international and domestic-only new ventures to see the strength of difference in the relationship between immigrant status and firm growth under these two strategies, and (2) between immigrant-founded and native-founded new ventures to see the strength of difference in the relationship between internationalization strategy and firm growth under these two founder types. The results of these analyses are presented in the Appendix C.

Table 12: Test of H3b: Ordinary Least Square (OLS) Estimate of Firm Growth

Estimators→ Variables ↓	β	St. Dev	t	p>|t|
Immigrant Status	1.694	1.518	1.12	0.266
Early International	0.705	0.792	0.89	0.374
Early International* Immigrant Status	-4.180**	1.802	-2.32	0.021
Male	0.700	0.736	0.95	0.342
Education	0.026	0.187	0.14	0.889
Prev. Industry Experience	-0.034	0.027	-1.24	0.218
Prev. Startup Experience	0.113	0.133	0.85	0.398
Internet Sales	0.621	0.667	0.93	0.353
Intellectual Property	1.175	0.933	1.26	0.209
Log(Total Assets_2 $)	0.695**	0.301	2.30	0.022
VC Funded	2.654	1.781	1.49	0.138
Tech Generator Industry	-0.513	0.543	-0.95	0.346
R&D Focus	-0.004	1.460	-0.00	0.998
Sales Focus	-0.876	0.997	-0.88	0.380
Log (Sales_2 $)	-1.633***	0.569	-2.87	0.005
High -Tech Center	-0.504	0.456	-1.11	0.269
Constant (α)	12.833***	4.663	2.75	0.006
F Statistics	1.06			
R2	0.187			
N	221			

Results on the Effect of Immigrant Status on Firm Growth for International versus Domestic-only New Ventures

First, examining only international new ventures, I find that (see Table C.1 in Appendix C) that *immigrant status* has a non-significant negative effect on firm growth for international new ventures. Second, examining only domestic-only new ventures, I find that (see Table C.2 in Appendix C) *immigrant status* has a non-significant positive effect on the sales growth of domestic-only new ventures. In order to test the significance of this difference, I calculated marginal fixed effects for immigrant status in each of the subsample (international and domestic-only new ventures). These values are presented in the last rows both in Table C.1 and Table C.2 in appendix C. I then conduct a two sample t-test to test if the marginal fixed effects of immigrant status on firm sales growth in the sample of international new ventures and domestic-only new ventures are significantly different from each other.

Figure 5: Moderating Effect of Early Internationalization Strategy on the Relationship between Founders' Immigrant Status and Firm Growth

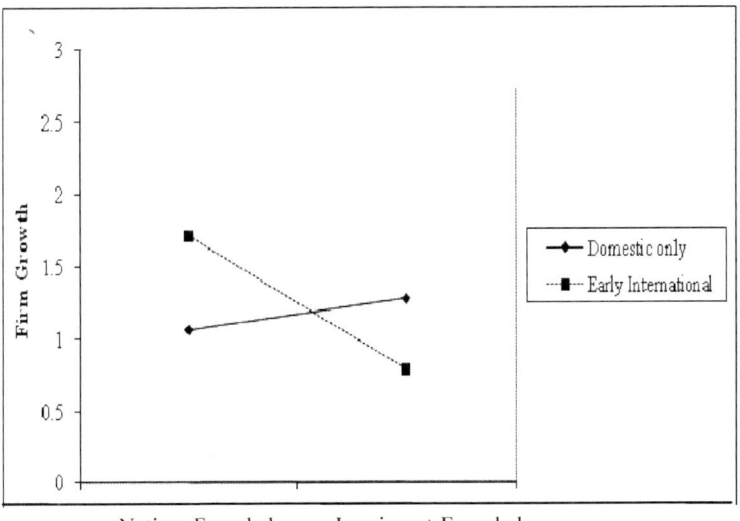

The result shows that the effect of immigrant status on firm sales growth is significantly different in the sample of international versus domestic-only new ventures with $t=-1.88$, $p<0.05$, providing statistical support for H3b although the effect is not in the direction that was hypothesized. Figure 5 presents the results graphically. It shows that for domestic-only new ventures, founders' immigrant status has no statistically significant effect on the probability of firm growth while for early internationalized new ventures, founders' immigrant status has a negative effect on the probability of firm growth.

Results on the Effect of Early Internationalization on Firm Growth for Immigrant versus Native-Founded New Ventures

First, examining solely immigrant-founded new ventures, I find that (See Table C.3 in appendix C) *early internationalization* has a negative and significant effect on firm sales growth with t = -2.55, p<0.05, contradicting H3b. It means that early internationalization strategy negatively affects firm growth for immigrant- founded new ventures. Second, examining only native-founded new ventures, I find that (See Table C.4 in Appendix C) *early internationalization* strategy has no significant effect on the sales growth for native-founded new ventures.

Figure 6: Moderating Effect of Founders' Immigrant Status on the Relationship between Early Internationalization Strategy and Firm Growth

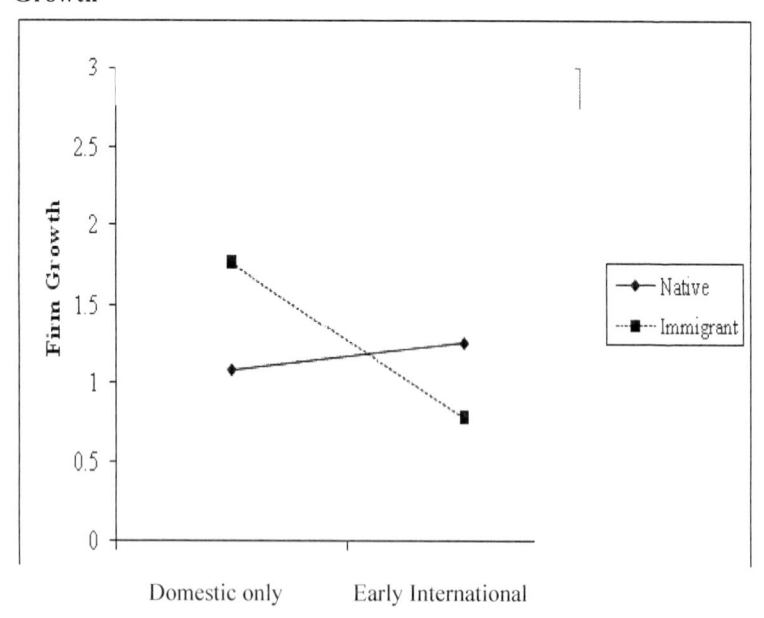

In order to test the significance of this difference, I calculated marginal fixed effects for immigrant status in each of the subsample (immigrant and native-founded new ventures). These values are presented in the last rows both in Table C.3 and Table C.4 in Appendix

C. I then conduct a two sample t-test to test if the marginal fixed effects of early internationalization on firm sales growth in the sample of immigrant and native-founded new ventures are significantly different from each other. The result shows that the effect of immigrant status on firm survival is significantly different in the sample of immigrant versus native-founded new ventures with t=-2.66, p<0.000, providing contradicting evidence for H3b. Figure 6 presents the results graphically. It shows that for native-founded new ventures; early internationalization strategy has no statistically significant effect on the probability of firm growth while for immigrant-founded new ventures; early internationalization strategy has a significant negative effect on the probability of firm growth.

Overall Summary of Results
This section describes the estimation results for each of the dependent variables. In all of the models, the omitted category is native-founders. First, I use a logit regression to test whether founders' immigrant status influences early internationalization of new ventures. I found a significantly positive effect of immigrant status on early internationalization at 10 % level. Thus, there is some, albeit weak, empirical support for Hypothesis 1.

Second, I provide the empirical results for the Hypothesis 2a, the effect of early internationalization on firm survival. I run an ivprobit regression where I use main industrial activity as an instrumental variable in the first stage. I found a significant and negative effect of early internationalization on firm survival at the 10% level. Thus, there is an empirical support for Hypothesis 2a. Next, I use a 2SLS estimate (ivreg) model to test Hypothesis 2b that early internationalization has a positive effect on firm growth but found no statistically significant effect of early internationalization on firm growth, although the direction of the relationship is positive, which is consistent with Hypothesis 2b.

Then, I provide the results for Hypothesis 3a that predict an interaction effect between immigrant status and early internationalization on firm survival. To test this hypothesis, I run an ivprobit regression on the whole sample with an interaction term (immigrant status * early internationalization). But, this analysis did not reach convergence and did not a produce result. Given that simple probit regression analysis shows a negative and significant interaction effect between immigrant status and early internationalization on firm survival at the 5% level, I do subsample analyses on international versus domestic-only new ventures and immigrant-founded versus native-founded new ventures to test Hypothesis 3a. The results of the probit regression analysis on the subsamples show that there is no significant relationship between immigrant status and firm survival for domestic-only new ventures while there is a significant but *negative* relationship between immigrant status and firm survival at the 5% level for international new ventures.

Finally, I test Hypothesis 3b that predict an interaction effect between immigrant status and early internationalization on firm growth, I run a ivreg regression with an interaction term (immigrant status * early internationalization). This analysis produces non-significant result for the effect of the interaction term on firm growth. Given that simple OLS regression analysis produces a significant estimate for the effect of the interaction term on firm growth, I do subsample analyses on international versus domestic-only new ventures and immigrant-founded versus native-founded new ventures to test Hypothesis 3b. The results of the OLS regression analysis on the subsamples show that there is no significant relationship between immigrant status and firm growth for domestic-only new ventures while there is a significant but a *negative* relationship between immigrant status and firm growth at the 5% level for international new ventures.

In summary, I find support for Hypothesis 1 that immigrant status has a positive influence on the early internationalization of new ventures. I also find that early internationalization is negatively related to firm survival, supporting Hypothesis 2a. However, I found no significant result for the effect of early internationalization on firm growth although the direction of the relationship is positive, which is in line with Hypothesis 2b. Contrary to my expectation, I found that while immigrant status has no effect on firm survival and growth for domestic-only new ventures, immigrant status has a significant *negative* effect on firm survival and growth for international new ventures (Hypothesis H3a and H3b) (see Table 13).

Table 13: Summary Analysis of Results

	Expected Effect	Finding	Support
1a	Immigrant-founded new ventures are more likely to be international at or near their foundings compared to native-founded new ventures.	Significant and positive relationship between founders' immigrant status and the likelihood of early internationalizn.	Supported
2a	There is a significant main effect of early internationalization of new ventures on firm survival such that international new ventures will have a lower probability of survival than domestic-only new ventures.	Significant and negative relationship between early internationalizn. and firm growth.	Supported
2b	There is a significant main effect of early internationalization of new ventures on firm growth such that international new ventures will have a higher probability of growth than domestic-only new ventures.	Non-significant and positive relationship between early internationalizn. and firm growth.	Not Supported
3a	There is a significant and positive interaction effect between founders' immigrant status and early internationalization on firm survival	Significant and negative interaction effect between founders' immigrant status and early internationalizn. on firm survival	Not Supported
3b	There is a significant and positive interaction effect between founders' immigrant status and early internationalization on growth	Significant and negative interaction effect between founders' immigrant status and early internationalizn. on firm growth	Not Supported

Robustness of Results
Two dimensions that appear important checking for robustness on these results are different internationalization measures and different measures for founders' outsider status.

Robustness to different internationalization measure.
The results are robust to specifying early internationalization as early international sales intensity. International intensity is measured as a category variable to the question of "*In 2007 what percentages of your companies' total sales were to individuals, businesses, or governments outside the US?*" This is a five category variable where the categories are 1=less than 5%, 2=5%-25%, 3=26%-50%, 4=51%-75%, and 5=76%-100. This measure shows a new venture's degree of involvement or commitment based on sales. This operationalization of early international intensity (as foreign sales as a percentage of total sales) is also consistent with prior literature (Fernhaber, McDougall-Covin & Shepherd, 2009; Carpenter, Pollock & Leary, 2003).

The results are produced by using ordered probit regression estimation to re-test the Hypothesis 1 by using international intensity as the dependent variable. The results in Table 14 shows that the coefficient of founders immigrant status is positive and significant with z=1.76 p<0.10, meaning that new ventures with immigrant founders have higher foreign sales as a percentage of total sales compared to new ventures with native founders.

Robustness to different founders' outsider status measure
Immigrant entrepreneurs vary among themselves in their outsiderness. In order to provide additional empirical support to the theoretical mechanisms I have developed in the theory & hypotheses section, I also ran a subsample analysis on immigrant-founded new ventures and examine the sources of variances within this group in the propensity to internationalize. For this analysis, I have used *U.S. citizenship* and *founder age* as two indicators of immigrant entrepreneurs' embeddedness in their country of adoption. I also include whether the immigrant entrepreneur is *Asian* to examine the differential likelihood of internationalizing for entrepreneurs from Asian countries.

Table 14: Robustness Test: Ordered Probit Estimate of International Sales Intensity (% of Foreign Sales)

Estimators→ Variables ↓	β	St. Dev.	Z	p>|z|
Immigrant Status	**0.403***	**0.230**	**1.76**	**0.079**
Male	0.369	0.250	1.48	0.140
Education	0.008	0.049	0.17	0.867
Prev. Industry Experience	0.014*	0.008	1.88	0.060
Prev. Startup Experience	0.001	0.042	0.03	0.973
Providing Product	0.734***	0.217	3.38	0.001
Internet Sales	0.356**	0.174	2.05	0.040
Intellectual Property	0.290	0.189	1.54	0.124
R&D Focus	-0.298	0.228	-1.31	0.191
Sales Focus	-0.180	0.241	-0.75	0.454
Resource Mobility	0.842***	0.304	2.78	0.006
Log(Total Assets $)	0.073	0.050	1.48	0.139
VC Funded	0.597	0.485	1.23	0.218
Tech Generator Industry	-0.487**	0.207	-2.35	0.019
High -Tech Center	0.207	0.187	1.11	0.267
State Export Intensity	0.009	0.022	0.40	0.691
Log Likelihood	-253.330			
N	232			

Table 15 presents the results. Both U.S. citizenship and age have negative and significant coefficients with $z=-2.14$ $p<0.05$ and $z=-2.22$ $p<0.05$ respectively. It means that older immigrant entrepreneurs and immigrant entrepreneurs with U.S. citizenship are less likely to internationalize early than younger immigrant entrepreneurs and immigrant entrepreneurs without U.S. citizenship. These two results together provide empirical support for the idea that outsiderness encourages early internationalization. Older immigrant entrepreneurs and immigrant entrepreneurs with the U.S. citizenships are more likely to be embedded in their adopted country, making them less outsiders relative to their younger and non-U.S. citizen counterparts, and hence decrease the likelihood of early internationalization.

Table 15: Robustness Test. The Probit Estimate of Early Internationalization with Different Measures of Outsiderness

Estimators→ Variables ↓	Coefficient	St. Error	z	p>|z|
U.S. Citizen	-3.647**	1.707	-2.14	0.033
Age	-0.286**	0.129	-2.22	0.027
Asian	-5.154***	1.598	-3.22	0.001
Male	-6.001***	2.155	-2.79	0.005
Education	4.680***	1.197	3.91	0.000
Prev. Industry Experience	0.360***	0.134	2.70	0.007
Prev. Startup Experience	1.576***	0.542	2.91	0.004
Intellectual Property	-12.264***	3.979	-3.08	0.002
Log(Total Assets_2 $)	0.560 *	0.368	1.79	0.073
ROA_2	1.027	0.673	1.53	0.127
High -Tech Center	1.031	1.232	0.84	0.403
Constant (a)	-24.083***	7.446	-3.23	0.001
Log Likelihood	-9.547			
R2	0.937			
N	38			

Moreover, results in Table 15 shows that being Asian negatively affects early internationalization. This result is surprising to some extent in that Asian countries are very active in high-tech spaces, and one would expect that these entrepreneurs undertake early internationalization at higher rates. However, it is possible that given Asian entrepreneurs especially those from India and China have a strong positive stereotype being smart high-tech entrepreneurs in the U.S. (from my personal interviews, 2010), it might be that new ventures with Asian immigrant entrepreneurs are more easily accepted and integrated as legitimate players in the U.S. As a result they might perceive a lower degree of outsiderness, which might in turn decrease their likelihood of early internationalization.

An interesting result that Table 15 presents is the negative and significant effect of gender on early internationalization of immigrant-founded new ventures with z=-3.22, p <0.001. This means that new ventures with female immigrant entrepreneurs are more likely to internationalize early than new ventures with male immigrant entrepreneurs. Another interesting finding is the negative and significant effect of intellectual property on early internationalization for immigrant-founded new ventures with z=-3.08 p<0.05. It might be that intellectual property might compensate some of the disadvantages of outsiderness in the adopted country such limited access to local networks to get resources, and encourage immigrant entrepreneurs with intellectual property to stay domestic-only very early on.

Finally, results in Table 15 shows that firm size and prior performance has a positive influence on early internationalization of immigrant-founded new ventures. This means that well-performing immigrant-founded new ventures are more likely to internationalize. This finding helps eliminate the argument that poor performing immigrant-founded new ventures are more likely to internationalize because they have nothing to lose by internationalizing that they are already doing badly.

CHAPTER 7
Field Interviews

In this chapter, I present my observations from the field interviews that I have conducted with insider and outsider entrepreneurs. In these interviews, I did not intend to test any research hypothesis. Instead, my objective was to explore the similarities and differences between high technology new ventures that are founded by insiders versus those founded by outsider entrepreneurs in order to get a deeper understanding about these companies that cannot be easily quantified (Maxwell, 1996). Therefore, it is important to note that the findings presented in this chapter are not generalizable. They represent my personal impressions that are used to enrich the theory and the premises of the study, and to shed a better light on some of the findings from my quantitative analyses (Yin, 2002).

I interviewed the primary founders of ten new ventures, of which five are immigrant entrepreneurs and five are native entrepreneurs. The descriptions of the cases are given in Table 16. All these ventures are operating in high technology industries ranging from web-design to high-tech agricultural products. All companies are located in Minnesota. These companies are chosen to ensure that all ventures are producing high technology or cutting-edge products or services while they vary in the immigrant status of their founders and their international strategies. This is done to more clearly observe the similarities and differences between new ventures on these dimensions. Moreover, these new ventures are selected such that they were all started in the U.S. so that they all face the same home country environment.

Table 16: Description of the Cases

	Immigrant-Founded	Native-Founded
Founders' Country of Origin	India (3), Turkey (2).	U.S. (5).
Founders' Citizenship	U.S. Citizens (3), Non-U.S. Citizens (2).	U.S. Citizens (5).
Gender of the Founder	Male (5).	Male (5).
Age of the Founder	Ranges from 35 to 65.	Ranges from 33 to 57.
Firm Age	Ranges from 3 to 9 years old.	Ranges from 4 to 8 years old.
Firm's Main Location	Minnesota (5)	Minnesota (5)
Number of employees	Ranges from 3 to 300.	Ranges from 1 to 130.
Sectors	Online work training, Online teleconferencing software, Watering system, Iphone application, Web design.	High-tech agricultural products, Security systems, Web design, Financial consulting, Aluminum Molding.
International Strategy	International (3), Domestic-only (2).	International (3), Domestic-only (2).
Number of countries entered	Two (1), three (1), five (1).	Two (1), three (1), nine (1)
Interviewed	Founder and CEO (5).	Founder and CEO (5).
Interview Method	Face-to-face (5).	Face-to-face (5).
Interview Duration	60 to 90 minutes.	60 to 90 minutes.
Interview Date	Feb – Nov, 2010	Feb – Nov, 2010

Interview Process

I have used *McCracken's Four-Step Method of Inquiry (1990)* as guidance to conduct my interviews and make sense of the data. In this method, the first stage involves a review of the analytic categories

Field Interviews

wherein the researcher is expected to do an exhaustive review of literature to deconstruct that literature in order to sharpen his/her capacity for surprise and to manufacture distance (*McCracken*, 1990). Before I conducted my interviews I did an extensive review of the literatures on immigrant entrepreneurship, international entrepreneurship, and international business and started to develop my working hypotheses about the strategies, and performance, of immigrant and native-founded new ventures. I developed my interview questions on the basis of this literature review, and on the theoretical relationships I had in mind.

The second stage in *McCracken*'s method involves a review of cultural categories with the aim of identifying associations, assumptions and expectations related to the topic of interest. In my case, I found this review especially important because I am an immigrant myself, and I have a deep intellectual familiarity with entrepreneurs and the issues that they face. Therefore, before going to interviews, I tried to make my associations, assumptions and expectations as explicit as I could by clearly writing down my premises and hypotheses. I did this in order to establish some sort of distance so that I would not take any information from my informants for granted but would increase my awareness of any new pieces of information.

The third stage in this method requires the discovery of cultural categories by implementing the interview itself. I conducted all interviews myself. Seven of the ten interviews took place at the physical sites of these companies, and the rest took place at the Carlson School of Management, University of Minnesota. The duration of the interviews ranged from one hour to one and a half hours. During the interviews, I followed a semi-structured approach. I predetermined about twenty questions based on my review of the literature, and organized these questions into four main types (See Appendix D for the full list of the questions). These types were (1) personal demographic questions, including founders' age, education, years spent in the U.S.; (2) firm specific questions, including the company's products and services, motivation to start the business, sources of financing, and firm resource configurations; (3) international strategy questions, including the firm's plans and actions regarding internationalization, countries entered, and mode of entry; and (4) performance questions, including perceived performance, and the role internationalization/non-internationalization in it.

When asking questions, I intentionally inquired for specific examples and experiences to learn about critical incidents to get more insight about the characteristics of insider and outsider founders and the characteristics of their companies. As for the sequence of my questions, I tried to pass from one topic to the next in a natural fashion; therefore, the sequence of the questions during each interview varied. Moreover, I permitted them to probe far beyond to my standard questions. Having this flexibility to respond to emergent insights gave me an opportunity to better understand the phenomenon (Berg, 1993). I looked for key concepts and surprises. Lastly, I tried to uncover important and surprising things by asking further probing questions.

As for the fourth stage, to draw conclusions about what an immigrant versus a native-founded high technology company looks like, strategizes, operates and performs, I wrote half a page to one page reflections of the interview after each interview. I jotted down the new insights, and the things that either surprised me or clearly confirmed my prior beliefs. All interviews were taped and afterwards were transcribed by a professional transcriber. I read each interview at least twice, and I compared and contrasted my interviews to derive meaningful conclusions regarding the similarities and differences between outsider and insider founded new ventures. Table 17 lists the six themes that have emerged from my evaluation of the data.

The Profile of Outsider Entrepreneurs and their Ventures
High need for achievement:
The main motivation for the outsider entrepreneurs to start their own businesses is the high need for achievement. Outsider entrepreneurs came to the U.S. to be successful and starting a successful company is a way of achieving this success. Although four out of five outsider entrepreneurs whom I interviewed have started their careers in big companies to achieve this success, the limited advancement opportunities in these companies were the main reason why they left these companies and started their own high technology businesses. For example, an Indian entrepreneur, Mr. M, explains why he left a national bank and went on starting his own company:

Field Interviews

Table 17: Profile of Outsider versus Insider Entrepreneurs and their New Ventures

Themes	Immigrant	Native
Reason to start	-High need for achievement -Limited upward mobility in large established companies	-Desire for autonomy -Belief that they can do things better than are done in established companies.
Pursuit of opportunities	-Divergent attention -Pursuit of many opportunities at once.	-Focused attention -Pursuit of one single opportunity at once.
Scalability of the business	-Scalability of the business from Day 1. -Start big. Do things only if they are scalable.	-Grow slowly but surely. Do not think about the scalability at the start. -Just start to do things. If it becomes scalable, great. If not, seems like no problem.
Mindset	-Global mindset -No differentiation between home and abroad. Anything anywhere that makes the most profit. -Globe is the market place.	-Local mindset -Clear distinction between home and abroad. -Some fear and reluctance to fully internationalize very quickly. -More careful and cautious approach. -Take it step by step.

Table 17: Profile of Outsider versus Insider Entrepreneurs and their New Ventures (continued)

Themes	Immigrant	Native
Product	-Consciously think about the world market. -Customized products for the world market from Day 1.	-Think about the local needs first. -Adjust for the world market when the time comes.
Country selection	-Preference for their home country if the opportunity is also there. Otherwise, it is where the opportunity is. -No concern mentioned about the institutional context.	-Opportunity-based -Institutional environment is important for country selection.

I was treated well and everything was going great [in the bank]. I was getting a good salary but I wasn't being promoted. What I found was, I was the diversity candidate. At that point of time no banks had employed diversity candidates. So all the banks were under pressure through a congressional ruling that they had to take diversity candidates. I found out that I was their best diversity candidate. And I was doing a good job, making a good salary, but I was not moving anywhere. In the four years I transferred to five different jobs. Everywhere there was a big problem and hot potato, take him in; he does the job. So that's basically what I did. Any department that had a problem, I'm there. He'll come fix it; he'll take care of it. So when I found out what was going on and why I was never promoted, I went to the senior management. In fact, it was the very senior management who interviewed me right out of school. I said, "What the heck is going on?" So I said, "I think it's time to think about this. Tell me what you have planned for me. I can't survive this. People that joined with me as a BA from the

Field Interviews

business school are already managers and one of them already an assistant vice president and I am not even a manager." Although I was making more money than a manager, I'm not being given that role to manage our department. I was a leader but I was not a manager. There is a difference between the two. So I said, "I think I'm going to leave." That's what I did, and I became independent.

An important reason for their high need for achievement and success is the feeling of pressure for success because they do not want to disappoint those whom they left behind and they are afraid of lagging behind among other immigrants from their home country in the U.S. Another Indian entrepreneur, Mr. R, explains this as follows:

> Immigrants are more focused on being successful because they, in a sense, left everything behind. So they can't go back and say, "I didn't succeed.

This high need for achievement and success seems to lead them to be more aggressive in their pursuit of opportunities. They do not want to miss any good opportunity. In that sense, they give a lot of attention to their external environment to spot and exploit new opportunities. While they are running their own business, they constantly scan the environment and learn from their friends, colleague, and competitors about the new possibilities either to open up a new business or to grow the existing ones. This aggressive opportunity seeking attitude is coupled by their desire for scalability and growth. In other words, immigrant entrepreneurs are in business to establish something big, they are not interested in building a life style business. Therefore, they consciously think about how to scale their business from Day 1. For example, a Turkish immigrant entrepreneur, Mr. H, says:

> I evaluate many opportunities and look for scalability in these opportunities, whether I will be able to grow it. If not, it means the opportunity is not for me.

Scalability of the Business:
Thinking big is also reflected in how they think about the market scope of their businesses. Immigrant entrepreneurs have a broader outlook, or a worldview, from the day they start their businesses. The demarcations across nations do not seem to be a relevant consideration for them when they evaluate a new business opportunity. They see the world as their market place, and they are eager to do business in whichever part of the world that is economically the most profitable. Because of this global outlook, they also design their products such that their products are easily customizable to the needs and requirements of different markets. Here is an excerpt from an Indian software entrepreneur, Mr. M, who explains how he thinks about product design:

> When you think about a business and you want to go international with it, you know that you have to design your product so that it can do multiple languages, right? So you design your products with what we call unicord so that it can do multiple languages. Otherwise, you do a product design completely English only, and then three years down the road when your product is really hitting the market, oh, this cannot do multiple design. So now come back and restart from zero. That's a large undertaking. Those are things that you need to take care of in the very beginning in your design of the product. It's like, if you make a widget, you need to know that the rest of the world is metric. This is the only place that is not metric. So the widget needs to fit the metric as well as this. So when you make the widget, you say, okay, I'm not going to make it only for the U.S. market, so I have to have two machines where I can either do metric or British. Or I have one machine that can do either/or. So that's a design element you have to bring in.

Any Country with Good Opportunity:
In terms of country selection, immigrant entrepreneurs seem to be naturally attracted to their home countries to do business, but this attraction does not seem to change their economic decision criteria when making entry decisions. That is, they prefer to operate in their

home countries only if these economies are also providing them with the economically best business opportunities. For example, an Indian entrepreneur who is in the online adult training business explains how he made his decision to enter India, his home country, and to other countries:

> Clearly there is an attraction [to home country]. It happens to be that the opportunity [at his home country] also is very large. In my case it happened to be coincidental. But India has 540 million people under 25, which is more than the rest of the world combined. Not quite, but 1/3 of the world are youth population, and they are the people who need training. So why wouldn't I be in India? That happens to be also where I am from. So they are both. If I were from Sri Lanka, I would have to think about whether I want to be in India or not, and I would probably be in India.

He continues:

> In my case they coincide. But I had no connections in Greece, I had no connections in Brazil, so we went there because the opportunity is there. In my previous life, I worked for National Car Rental system, we didn't go to India. We went to 114 countries, but India was one of the last because that's not where the opportunity was.

Selective Financing:
In order to finance their business, immigrant entrepreneurs mainly rely on friends, families, and business angels. They believe these sources of financing give them more control over their business relative to other sources of financing. Moreover, while getting external financing, outsider entrepreneurs are not only after money but also after connections that these sources might provide them. Indeed, they believe that getting money is no problem but getting connections is the heart of the matter. One of the Indian entrepreneurs, Mr. G, explains this as follows:

If you look at the money economy right now, there is a lot of money floating around. If you want to get money, you get money. The problem is, to be able to use that money in an effective manner, you need contacts. So I don't want money from somebody who doesn't have contacts. So if I'm getting formal money from somebody, whether it's venture capitalists or incubators or angels, I would not go to anybody who does not have contacts, because you are given the money, you are giving them a stake, but it doesn't help in the company anyway. Yes, I might be begging at that point, but it doesn't help in the success of the company. The biggest thing that a startup needs, particularly like this, is contacts. If they have contacts in a research firm, if they have contacts, are a doctor—something I want more than money. It's amazing how many times people have approached me and said, 'Oh, you are the founder of this company? Do you need money?' People here, venture capitalists in the U.S., when they came to know this, 'Do you need money?

Surprisingly, immigrant entrepreneurs seem not to have any problems getting external financing from angel investors or venture capitalists. In fact, they think that being an immigrant is actually an advantage to get these sources of financing because of the increasing number of immigrants who are VCs and angel investors in the U.S., and the positive stereotypes that high technology immigrant entrepreneurs have in the eyes of all stakeholders. Also, immigrant entrepreneurs seem to be very selective of their sources. For example, an Indian high-tech entrepreneur, Mr R, puts it as follows:

> You look at the VC markets, you look at the private equity market, and there are a disproportionate number of immigrants in those. They ask "You need money? We're ready to invest." We go, "No, sorry, we don't want money unless you are bringing something to the table. Either you bring contacts, either you bring name brand. Something you should bring more than money." Otherwise, no need. In fact, my friend who is

running the company, he has turned down many, many people who are coming with open wallets.

On the other hand, getting bank financing seems to be tougher because of the perception of the bank towards immigrant entrepreneurs. For example, an Indian high-tech entrepreneur, Mr. M, explains the treatment he got from a bank as follows:

> My color is brown. That's a giveaway. Somebody looks at you, and that color, they immediately know I am from India. So all the stereotypes fall into place. That is a big difficulty for me to remove that obstacle. I have to clear that big screen, and then get entry. That is always there. That is a big disadvantage. If I want to get a loan from the bank, I walk into the manager. [makes gesture] You know? I have to have a friend who will refer me there. Otherwise, if I just walk in, "Where the heck is he coming from? Who is he?" I only know that I have been a citizen of this country for so long. They don't know that. Unfortunately, I am this color, and that gives something away, so it is tough; it is difficult. It is extra difficult.

So, it seems like external financiers are not homogenous in their attitudes towards outsider entrepreneurs. While VCs and angel investors have a positive stereotype for high-tech immigrant entrepreneurs, and they are extra willing to finance their ventures, banks have a negative serotype and they are less likely to provide financing. Therefore, immigrant entrepreneurs deliberately stay away from bank financing. If they have to, their strategy is to use personal credit cards to finance their businesses rather than applying for direct credit for their businesses.

As for their resource configurations, immigrant entrepreneurs are very careful in terms of how they invest their money. The do not invest in anything unless it has direct value added to the business and contributes to its growth. Product development and sales are the two functions with special importance. It looks like having to decide how to allocate resources to these two functions gives immigrant entrepreneurs the hardest time. They avoid investing in areas other than these two.

Moreover, there is a noticeable tendency to avoid buying assets if these assets are rentable or leasable.

The Profile of Insider Entrepreneurs and their Ventures
Need for autonomy:
The main motivation for the insider entrepreneurs to start a business is the desire for autonomy. Four out of five four out of five insider entrepreneurs whom I interviewed have worked for big companies in the U.S. They believed that these companies were too unwieldy to get things done, and their limited ability to change the status quo in these companies was the main reason they left these companies and started their own high technology businesses. For example, an insider entrepreneur, Mr. C, explains why he left his prior company he was working for and went on starting his own company:

> I was in the industry, I was tired of traveling, I was tired of things being run really poorly, I saw where the big corporation I was working for was making all kinds of mistakes, and things that from the outside just looked really dumb why you would do something that way. It just didn't make sense. You know, there are political reasons internally. There are all these politics that get in the way of doing the right thing. I think for me it was looking at those politics and going, what if you had a place, and you took all the politics and boundaries out of the way and just focused on really doing the work for clients, I think ultimately you could build a much better business. And that's how we came about.

Another insider entrepreneur, Mr. D, explains why he left his company after the business unit he was a part in his old company was sold to GE.

> We had eventually built the business up and it got acquired by General Electric, and it became G.E. Security. After a while it just wasn't fun anymore. Obviously, you know who G.E. is, but it's a very matrix oriented company. So it just wasn't fun. We saw the opportunity because we thought they were goofing it up even though we ran a big chunk of it, my co-founder and

Field Interviews

I. We thought corporate-wide they were goofing up, so we decided to strike out and try it on our own.

The dissatisfaction with their prior employers' way of doing business leads insider entrepreneurs to start their own businesses and perfect them. Therefore, insider entrepreneurs are very focused in their attention and they give limited attention to the opportunities outside of their domain. They are very meticulous in what they do. They take things step by step and evaluate each step carefully. In that sense, they want to start small and grow slowly and surely. This full concentration on their business is coupled by an insular mindset. They are not willing to extend the scope of their businesses very quickly. In fact, they even show some sort of resistance to it. For example, insider entrepreneur, Mr. C., explains this as follows:

> I think you could easily spread yourself too thin. You could overinvest in one market, and that could cripple you to lose money to then weaken your initial stance. So I think that the risk side of it is probably the highest one from a resource investment standpoint.

Domestic Focus:
Moreover, it is noticeable that insider entrepreneurs seem to be more sympathetic to internationalization when they believe internationalization will strengthen their position domestically. In that sense, even when they do international business, they have a domestic emphasis. In addition, insider entrepreneurs perceive a clear distinction between home county and abroad, and they have a cautious attitude toward internationalization. Although they are open to do idea of doing business abroad, they clearly perceive greater risks in international markets and they prefer to take it step by step. For example, an insider entrepreneur, Mr. W, states that:

> For me it [internationalization] doesn't make sense at this point. I have thought that in the future there could be some things that we could do possibly in Asia. I have thought about that, but that would be five or ten years down the road, and I

would need to have somebody who is probably from that area but happens to be living here, to really kind of start reaching out into those areas. Because I have to stabilize my business here, I think, first, and get enough experience here that I can start to build it out. Eventually I would like to do work in other states, so I don't see what I'm doing as just doing work here, but actually my longer-term vision is to grow into other states, and if an opportunity came along, to do that internationally.

Countries with Strong Institutions:
Insider entrepreneurs are also very careful in their country selection choices. They emphasize the institutional environment of the host countries as an important consideration in their country selection. They prefer to do business in those countries with strong legal systems, stable governments, and no social turmoil. For example, Mr. P. explains how he decided between Brazil and Chile as follows:

> Although it had a greater market, it was difficult to do business in Brazil. We have a very simple way of doing business. We help each other and everybody makes money, in general. It's very simple. In Brazil it was different. In Chile what we see is a stable government. We don't see any issues on corruption that we would potentially see in other parts of South America.

While insider entrepreneurs are more cautious in their internationalization decisions and selection of the markets in which they sell their products, they seem to be more comfortable when it comes to outsourcing their production activities abroad. India and China are their top choices. Surprisingly, it was noticeable that insider entrepreneurs talk about their outsourcing activities to India and/or China as a natural or taken for granted way of doing business to cut costs. It seems like outsourcing design and/or manufacturing functions to these countries has become an industry standard in high technology industries.

Similarities between Outsider and Insider Entrepreneurs and their Ventures

I observe many similarities between insider and outsider entrepreneurs and their high technology new ventures. First, both insider and outsider founded new ventures tend to prefer "B to B" (business to business) business model rather than "B to C" (business to consumers) business model. New ventures are in need of investing in distribution channels and mass advertising to effectively serve real consumers. However, they lack financial, human and other resources to do these investments. Therefore, they tend to market their products to the next player in the distribution channel rather than going all the way through to the end consumer.

A second similarity is their reluctance to make investments in areas that do not have direct value added to the business. For example, new ventures with both outsider and insider founders tend to avoid investing in land, office space or additional employees if these things do not directly contribute to the value of the product, and to its sales. The most difficult decision they seem to make every day is the allocation of resources between R&D and marketing. They all agree that these two areas are essential for the success of their ventures and they struggle to decide between investing in R&D to make their products better to persuade customers to buy them versus investing in persuading customers to buy their existing products.

A third observed similarity is that both insider-founded and outsider-founded new ventures target niche markets and avoid direct competition with large established companies both domestically and internationally. They focus on those markets that are passed over by big companies, and many times they choose to cooperate with big companies rather than competing with them. They cooperate by supplying inputs to them, by forming alliances or making licensing or other type of cooperative arrangements. Many times, they also benefit from these companies to distribute their products along the value chain to the end customers.

A finally striking similarity between outsider and insider founded new ventures is their approach to outsourcing R&D or production to other countries, especially to India and China. Both types of new ventures state the importance and relevance of outsourcing their R&D

or production for cost cutting purposes. They believe that, given their limited resources, outsourcing is not an option anymore but a must. More importantly, they perceive outsourcing as a taken for granted way of doing business in high technology industries, almost as an industry norm. Both types of new ventures tend to prefer India for outsourcing R&D and China for outsourcing manufacturing.

Differences between Outsider versus Insider Entrepreneurs and their Ventures

As explained in more detail above, I observe many differences between outsider and insider entrepreneurs and their high technology ventures. First, while outsider entrepreneurs are primarily motivated by high need for achievement, insider entrepreneurs are largely motivated by the need for autonomy to start their own companies. While outsider entrepreneurs leave their prior employees and decide to start their own company due to limited upward mobility, insider entrepreneurs leave their prior employers because they believe that they can do things much better themselves than they were doing in their old companies.

Another important difference between outsider and insider entrepreneurs is that outsider entrepreneurs have divergent attentions and they tend to follow many opportunities at once, while insider entrepreneurs have a more focused attention and tend to pursue one opportunity at a time. For example, an insider entrepreneur Mr. C. explains this difference between himself and his Indian co-founder Mr. S as follows:

> I think he [his Indian co-founder] is more opportunity oriented. Opportunity is another way of saying, "Look over here, there may be an opportunity" versus me saying, "Yeah, but that could dilute what we have here." As we talked earlier, you can only put so many investments in so many pools. He was trying to put more seeds out there. Do you know what I mean?

He adds:

> It's investment strategy. I think he thinks that you can put ten seeds, and nine will grow. My thing is that if you put ten seeds,

Field Interviews

and you have ten drops of water and water each seed with one drop, none of them may grow, right?

A third important difference is related to the scalability of the business. Insider entrepreneurs believe that as long as they do things right, the business will grow naturally and even if it does not, it is not a problem for them. For outsider entrepreneurs, on the other hand, one of the objectives in starting a new business is starting something big; they would not start a business that would stay small. An insider entrepreneur Mr. C. explains this difference between himself and his Indian co-founder Mr. S as follows:

> I think, he [his Indian co-founder] was more looking at the mechanics of how it's built so it's scalable from Day 1. He would say what would this look like if we did it there, what if we open another office, could we move it down there? Could we open an office in another state? He's always looking to how we get our foot somewhere else and keep it going. I've been of the feeling that you can put ten drops of water on one seed and you've got a better likelihood of a high growth, a stronger growth, than ten seedlings that may not weather it through the summer.

The reason behind this difference seems to be different pressures for success for insider and outsider entrepreneurs. While for insider entrepreneurs, success is self-defined, and as long as they are happy, there is no reason to necessarily grow their businesses, while for outsider entrepreneurs, they feel the pressure for success not only internally but also externally both from their peers in the adopted country, and from people whom they left behind in their home country. Therefore, they want to accomplish big things to prove that they are successful. Mr. C. explains this difference as follows:

> I don't have the pressure to care what people think of succeeding or not. I go after my own success. I'm like, Hey, this is great, we're doing good. I don't need a double down when we're doing good. Let's grow it 20% now. We're solid.

How much do you need? I think for me I could look at what do I need personally financially sometimes. He [his Indian co-founder] may look at what his objective is, what is he trying to grow, what are the pressures on himself for success? Differently from me, my pressure for success is a different definition than theirs. Their pressure for success is to be successful and to see themselves as successful. Mine is to succeed and to say, "Hey, I started a business, I can pay my bills, I've done better than where I was before," whereas I think their pressure of success is, "I've succeeded, I've met my goals." It's a less tangible one and it's more of an emotional personal stress. The other one is a very tangible one—I'm not going into foreclosure on my home. So there are different pressures, I think, one from the other.

Another importance difference between outsider and insider entrepreneurs is how different financiers evaluate outsider and insider entrepreneurs, and how insider and outsider entrepreneurs evaluate different sources of financing. First, while formal traditional financiers such as banks and government organizations still discriminate against outsider entrepreneurs relative to insider entrepreneurs, VCs and angel investors seem to have positive stereotype of outsider entrepreneurs and favor outsider entrepreneurs. This positive image of high-tech immigrant entrepreneurs is partly spread by the media and partly because of the increasing number of immigrants as VCs and angel investors. For example, an insider entrepreneur, Mr. C. explains how his Indian co-founder fits this positive stereotype and how this helped their venture get external resources:

> I think people outside even more so when we started perceived us differently. I think one is there's him being Indian there's obviously an idea of, oh, look, they're Indian; they must know computers. There is some stigma, especially in our niche, IT world. I think at some level people outside perceive that as the thing that that brought some legitimacy. "Oh, they're a computer company. Look, that must be the

real braniac computer guy" It was just some perception. That helped.

An Indian entrepreneur Mr. T says:

> You look at the VC markets, you look at the private equity market, and there are a disproportionate number of immigrants in those.

In terms of the evaluation of the sources of financing, while insider entrepreneurs are primarily after money, outsider entrepreneurs seem to require financiers to bring business contacts and other types of value added other than just money. For example, a native entrepreneur Mr.D explains their approach to get financing:

> When you are scrambling for money, you're willing to take it from anybody who's not a crook, you know.

An outsider entrepreneur Mr. T explains how he evaluates different financing sources:

> You try to narrow down the sources to those who play in the area. Then it's simply a question of, what is it they are willing to value? What is it they are bringing to the party? Do they bring experience in that? Can they help you? There might be three or four players who are willing to put money at the same price. What else do they bring besides the money? Do they bring connections? In our case, it's very important that they bring international links. What do they bring besides the money? Do they have an experience base of people who build companies, or is it a fresh MBA out of school who is trying to tell us what to do and he doesn't know what the hell he's talking about?

Finally, outsider entrepreneurs seem to have a global mindset relative to insider entrepreneurs whose main focus are domestic markets. While outsider entrepreneurs plan their strategies, products and services to

102   *The Outsider Entrepreneurs*

serve to the world markets from very early on, insider entrepreneurs seem to focus being successful domestically even if they might have international operations in some cases. For example, an outsider entrepreneur Mr. T. explains the difference between insider and outsider entrepreneurs in their approach to global markets in the U.S.

> I think, in today's world, if you are a technology company and you don't have a global footprint, I think it's harder to get funding. I like the word you used, "born global." You have to be born global these days, especially if you are a technology company.

He adds:

> Because they [insider entrepreneurs] have so much business in this country that they don't ever think about going outside. The "World Series" is baseball between five cities of the U.S. That is not the idea of the world.

CHAPTER 8
Discussion of Findings

In this study, I examined the role of founders' outsider status in the early internationalization and performance of new U.S. high technology ventures. In doing this, I used the behavioral theory of the firm. I identified several gaps in the literature that this study is aimed to fill. First, while extant research in international entrepreneurship has provided valuable insights into the determinants and consequences of new venture internationalization, several questions remained to be answered regarding how being an outsider (or for that matter, an insider) in the country in which an entrepreneur starts his business relates to the international strategies of his venture and its performance. This study, therefore, set out to examine the differences between outsider and insider entrepreneurs and how these differences affect the decision to internationalize early, and the consequences of this decision in terms of firm survival and growth.

The second gap identified by this study concerns the literature on immigrant entrepreneurship. Research on immigrant-founded high technology startups are rare and the focus of the few existing studies have so far been on the determinants of the decision of highly skilled immigrant entrepreneurs to move into self-employment, or their contributions to the macro outcomes such as regional development or economic growth. Little research exists that examines the ways in which this value is being created. Specifically, our knowledge of the ways new ventures founded by outsider entrepreneurs strategize and perform relative to those founded by native entrepreneurs in high-technology industries is almost non-existent. This study, therefore, attempted to address this gap in the literature by examining the relationships between founders' outsider status, early internationalization and firm performance in high technology industries.

Finally, the theoretical perspectives explaining the activities of immigrant entrepreneurs (and the activities of foreign firms for that matter) have focused on the disadvantages that outsiders face relative to insiders. Several studies have argued that outsiders face greater institutional pressures relative to insiders due to their lack of familiarity with the institutional context, lack of social networks, and the discrimination that they face by institutional actors. This study has brought a new theoretical perspective to this issue by examining not only the negative but also the positive implications of outsiderness, and the contingencies that come with it, by taking a behavioral approach. Thus, in response to these gaps in the literature, in the context of high technology industries I asked three questions:

1. How does outsiderness versus insiderness (i.e., founders' immigrant status) affect early internationalization strategy?
2. How does early internationalization affect firm survival and firm growth?
3. How does outsiderness versus insiderness (i.e., founders' immigrant status) affect firm survival and firm growth for domestic-only and international new ventures?

In this chapter, I begin by interpreting the empirical results. I then discuss the contributions to theory and practice, and then I conclude with an assessment of the limitations of the study and suggest some directions for future research.

Discussion of Research Findings
The general hypothesis of this study is that founders' immigrant status has an effect on the early strategies of new ventures, and the effect of immigrant status on new venture performance depends on whether or not the venture is early internationalized. By drawing on the behavioral theory of the firm, I argued that because outsider entrepreneurs are more likely to possess global mindsets and lack of strong roots in their countries of adoption, they are more likely to build ventures that are

Discussion of Findings

international at or near their foundings relative to those ventures founded by insider entrepreneurs, who are more likely to be subject to domestic mindsets and strong local ties. Moreover, I argued that the outsider status of entrepreneurs conveys some disadvantages in setting up and operating businesses in their country of adoption, but that these challenges also provide immigrant entrepreneurs with a capacity to manage such difficulties in new foreign markets. Therefore, while immigrant-founded new ventures might be at a disadvantage and perform worse relative to native-founded new ventures domestically, this relationship is reversed for international new ventures; that is, immigrant-founded international new ventures perform better than native-founded international new ventures.

In line with my argumentation, I found empirical support for the hypothesis that new ventures with outsider founders are more likely to internationalize early. I also found that early internationalization as a strategy has a negative main effect on firm survival and a positive main effect on firm growth (although the latter is not statistically significant), supporting my argumentation. However, my moderation hypotheses are not supported, but instead the opposite effect was found. In particular, I found that *immigrant-founded international* ventures are, in fact, less likely to survive and grow than *native-founded international* new ventures, and that *immigrant-founded international* new ventures are less likely to survive and grow than *immigrant-founded domestic-only* new ventures.

Finding 1: New Ventures with Outsider Entrepreneurs were More Likely to Be International Relative to New Ventures with Insider Entrepreneurs

I find empirical evidence that new ventures founded by non-U.S. born entrepreneurs are more likely to have international sales early relative to new ventures founded by U.S. born entrepreneurs in U.S. high technology industries. This finding is consistent with the argument of this study that outsider entrepreneurs tend to have broader global perspectives and have less commitment to their adopted countries relative to native entrepreneurs.

Although Hypothesis 1 is supported, four possible alternative explanations may be behind the observation that the presence of an immigrant entrepreneur as the primary founder is positively associated with early internationalization: (a) Immigrant entrepreneurs might be more capable than native entrepreneurs because only the best or most qualified people are able to immigrate to the U.S. from their home countries; (b) Immigrant entrepreneurs might self-select into industries that are more global in nature, (c) Immigrant-founded new ventures might have greater resource availability through their international networks; and (d) Immigrant entrepreneurs might be subject to the "pull effect" of their home countries and that might be driving early internationalization. The available prior work and the available evidence in this study are used to address these mechanisms.

Capability of Entrepreneurs: The alternative mechanism is that highly skilled immigrant entrepreneurs are more capable than native entrepreneurs because only the best in their countries are able to migrate and start their own businesses in the U.S. While it is quite plausible that highly skilled immigrant entrepreneurs may be more capable than people in their countries of origin, it is not very plausible that they are also necessarily more capable than highly skilled native entrepreneurs in their country of adoption. In any case, it would be ideal to control for the unobserved ability of entrepreneurs, but this is hard to measure. Nonetheless, work on new ventures suggests that venture capitalists (VCs) tend to fund more capable entrepreneurs and new ventures (Eckhardt, Shane & Delmar, 2006). Therefore, to control for this explanation both VC financing and education are included as controls, and the result is that founders' immigrant status is still significant.

Industry Selection: The second alternative mechanism is the idea that highly skilled immigrant entrepreneurs may select to operate in industries that are more global in nature. Analyses were conducted to test the propensity of immigrant versus native entrepreneurs to self-select themselves in different industries within high technology realm. Results show that there is no statistically significant difference between immigrant and native entrepreneurs in their selection of industries that they operate in. Thus, it seems that industry selection does not explain the results.

Resource Availability: The third alternative mechanism is that immigrant-founded new ventures may have access to larger amounts of

Discussion of Findings

resources through their international networks, and, therefore are able to afford the costs of early internationalization and broader geographic market scope. Analyses were conducted to test the difference between immigrant-founded versus native-founded new ventures in terms of the magnitude of the starting total assets that they have had. Results show that there is no statistically significant difference, and in fact, in terms of absolute numbers, immigrant-founded new ventures had smaller amounts of total assets relative to native-founded new ventures. Thus, it seems that resource availability does not explain the results.

Home Country "Pull" Effect: Another alternative mechanism is that home country "pull effect" or existing knowledge about and social relations in their home countries incentivize immigrant entrepreneurs to do business with their home countries, and drive early internationalization of immigrant-founded new ventures. This explanation cannot be entirely ruled out because the Kaufmann Firm Survey does not include data regarding which countries new ventures are doing business in. Nonetheless, in order to address this issue with the data at hand, the analyses were re-run on the sample of domestic-only new ventures. In this analysis the geographic market scope of the new ventures within the U.S. is used as a dependent variable (See Appendix E).

Although it is very likely that early internationalization of immigrant-founded new ventures may, in part, be driven by the "pull effect" of their home countries, if this explanation were a big driver of immigrant-founded new ventures early internationalization, we would not necessarily expect immigrant-founded domestic-only new ventures would be significantly different from native-founded domestic-only new ventures in terms of their geographic market scope within the U.S. However, if the mechanism I am proposing in this study, that the early experiences of outsider entrepreneurs with personal mobility and their outsiderness cause them to suffer less from cognitive and relational barriers to early internationalization relative to native entrepreneurs, is correct, then it is reasonable to expect that new ventures with immigrant entrepreneurs also target a broader geographic market even within the U.S. relative to new ventures with native entrepreneurs.

The results presented in Appendix E provide support to eliminate the alternative explanation that early internationalization of immigrant-founded new ventures is driven by home country pull effect. These results show that domestic-only new ventures with immigrant entrepreneurs are significantly more likely to operate within a larger geographic market within the U.S. relative to domestic-only new ventures with native entrepreneurs. This result is consistent with the theoretical reasoning used to develop Hypothesis 1 that outsiderness enables immigrant entrepreneurs to evaluate a wider set of possible investment opportunities and to target wider geographic market within the U.S., as well as outside of the U.S., relative to high-tech insider entrepreneurs who are more locally embedded and therefore more limited in their pursuit of opportunities outside of their local market.

My analyses of qualitative interviews also support that immigrant entrepreneurs target broader markets. While native entrepreneurs put a particular emphasis on the domestic market, immigrant entrepreneurs perceive *"globe as their market place"* (An immigrant entrepreneur, Mr R.). Immigrant entrepreneurs I have interviewed also provides qualitative evidence that although home country connections are important to them, they make country selection choices based largely on the availability of market opportunities. For example, an Indian entrepreneur talks about his country selection process. He comments:

> Clearly there is an attraction [to India]. It happens to be that the opportunity [in India] also is very large. In my case it happened to be coincidental...So why wouldn't I be in India? That happens to be also where I am from. So they are both. If I were from Sri Lanka, I would have to think about whether I want to be in India or not, and I would probably be in India...But I had no connections in Greece, I had no connections in Brazil, so we went there because the opportunity is there. In my previous life, I worked for National Car Rental system, we didn't go to India. We went to 114 countries, but India was one of the last because that's not where the opportunity was.

Results from the test of Hypothesis 1 also indicate that while many factors offered in the prior literature for new venture internationalization are highly significant including education, firm size

Discussion of Findings

and internet sales, other factors such as gender, age, previous industry and startup experiences of founders turn out to be non-significant. Moreover, results from Hypothesis 1 show a positive and significant effect of resource mobility on new venture internationalization. This finding provides empirical evidence supporting the theoretical argument about the importance of structural resource characteristics for new venture internationalization. Gasmann & Keupp (2007: 352) state that:

> ....a study of an international new venture's resources would be the first step to arrive at an understanding of its capability to internationalize. Indeed, resources that enable the generation of capabilities are especially important to international new ventures. A venture's ability to enter foreign markets can be linked to its accumulated tangible and intangible resource stocks.

This suggests how new ventures configure their resources can enhance or inhibit their capability to enter foreign markets rapidly and achieve superior international performance. For example, Sapienza et al (2006) theoretically argued that the flexibility of the existing resources helps new ventures to shift their resources for alternative uses quickly and efficiently. In line with this argument, the significant result for the effect of resource mobility on early internationalization indicates that those new ventures with less locally embedded or committed resources may benefit from this flexibility when venturing abroad, or that ventures that intend to internationalize accumulate more mobile resources.

This argument is also consistent with the general claim of this study that low levels of commitment to their country of adoption gives outsider entrepreneurs an advantage to pursue early internationalization. In fact, results also show a positive and significant correlation between founders' immigrant status and the mobility of firm resources. That is, new ventures with outsider founders tend to have more mobile resources, may be as a preparation to take on an internationalization strategy. Because this result suggests a positive relationship between founders' immigrant status and early internationalization, it seems to provide additional support that substantiates the theoretical mechanism for the importance of flexibility for venturing abroad.

Despite the fact that my quantitative data indicates significant difference between native versus immigrant-founded new ventures in the mobility of their resource configurations, my qualitative analyses did not reveal such a difference. Instead, I observed a general tendency towards having mobile resources regardless of founders' immigrant status. Largely due to resource constraints, entrepreneurs in general avoid making hard to reverse, long-term commitments whenever possible. Instead, they prefer leasing and renting to buying, outsourcing to employing additional work-force. An immigrant interviewee illustrates this point below:

> I don't buy anything that I can rent because of limited resources. Why should I put it in things that I can use or rent or get on available cost basis?

Finding 2: Early Internationalization Negatively Affects Firm Survival

I find that firm early internationalization is negatively related to firm survival. International new ventures' rate of short term survival is lower than domestic-only new ventures' rate of short term survival. This result is in accordance with Hypothesis 2a, which states that internationalization presents a lot of uncertainties and risks for new ventures and decreases their probability of short term survival. These results substantiate the theoretical argument that new ventures are small in size and resources, and suffer from "liability of newness," therefore, their existence is vulnerable to uncertainties that international markets entail. This means that early internationalization is not necessarily a good strategy for resource limited new ventures, but a risky strategy with potential benefits. Moreover, results show a positive and significant effect of firm resources measured as total assets on firm survival. This result again signifies the importance of resource availability to overcome the difficulties and survive in the first years of their operations.

Another important empirical relationship is the significant and positive effect of founders' formal education on firm survival. Although prior studies did not produce consistent findings for the effect of education on firm performance, the results of this study indicate that regardless of whether the firm is domestic-only or international, founders' education has a significant and positive effect on new venture survival. This finding implies that formal education develops entrepreneurs' capacity to make better decisions, to allocate their resources more effectively. It is also possible that founders' formal education increases the legitimacy of new ventures in the eyes of stakeholders and contributes to new venture survival.

Finding 3: Early Internationalization does not Affect Firm Growth
I also find that early internationalization positively but non-significantly affects firm growth where firm growth is measured as the sales growth one year after internationalization. That is, international new ventures' sales growth is still higher than domestic-only new ventures' sales growth although this difference did not reach statistical significance. Although insignificant, the positive direction of the relationship between early internationalization and firm growth is in accordance with Hypothesis 2b and with the literature that states that internationalization provides new ventures with growth opportunities by opening up new markets with new consumers and technology. This result is also consistent with the prior literature and provides support for the idea that early internationalization is an important growth strategy for new ventures.

The current literature makes the theoretical argument that previous start up experiences help entrepreneurs learn about the process of starting up and operating new ventures, and that entrepreneurs benefit from this knowledge in their new businesses; therefore, prior start up experiences positively influence firm performance. Surprisingly, my results show that founders' previous start up experience significantly and negatively affects firm growth. One possible, albeit speculative, explanation for this unexpected finding might be the inability of some entrepreneurs to start successful businesses, and that those entrepreneurs might keep starting and failing many businesses.

These results on firm survival and growth together reflect the complexity of performance and indicate the importance of utilizing different indications of performance to fully assess the advantages and disadvantages of early internationalization. While results show a negative and significant effect of early internationalization on survival, a positive but non-significant effect is observed for the effect of early internationalization on firm growth conditional on surviving. These findings suggest that future studies should include other performance indicators, such as productivity, efficiency, and innovation, to get a better understanding of the differential performance effects of early internationalization strategy.

Finding 4: Early Internationalization Negatively Affects Firm Survival and Firm Growth for Immigrant-Founded New Ventures

The moderating effect of early internationalization strategy in the relationship between founders' immigrant status and firm survival (Hypotheses 3a) and between founders' immigrant status and surviving firms' growth (Hypotheses 3b) do not receive empirical support. Indeed, I find that while early internationalization strategy does not significantly relate to either survival or growth of native-founded new ventures, it is significantly and negatively related to both the survival and the growth of immigrant-founded new ventures.

Contemporary scholarly understanding of the effect of firm strategy on firm performance is that although different international strategies may have different performance implications, given that entrepreneurs' internationalization decisions are affected by their unique circumstances including, the characteristics of external environment, and the past performance of their ventures, it is that entrepreneurs are in fact the best strategy (whether it is staying domestic-only or internationalizing) given the attributes of their firms and their environments. In fact, if these firms had chosen a different strategy, they would have done even worse (Shaver, 1998). From this point of view, strategy alone should not have a significant effect on the performance of ventures when the special circumstances of each firm are taken into account.

The findings of this study confirm this perspective for native-founded new ventures. These ventures seem to make the right decision

Discussion of Findings

whether it is to remain domestic-only or early internationalize, and therefore, early internationalization strategy alone does not have significant effect on their survival or growth. Contrary to the expectations of this study, however, the findings show that early internationalization *decreases* the performance of immigrant-founded new ventures both in terms of survival and growth. These results suggest that immigrant entrepreneurs might suffer from systematic biases or pressures in making early internationalization decisions that result in subsequent poor performance.

One potential explanation might be "overconfidence". Immigrant entrepreneurs may develop overconfidence in their abilities to deal with the challenges of new foreign markets, and may take unwarranted risks. While native entrepreneurs may be acting more cautiously and make their evaluations more objectively, given the experience that they have had, immigrant entrepreneurs might be overconfident in what they can achieve and have and systematically overestimate their chances in new markets. Moreover, while native entrepreneurs might be more willing to receive new information and learn to evaluate their environments better, immigrant entrepreneurs may become ignorant and blind to the new information as they may think that they already know enough. This explanation might help interpret the overall results of the study that although immigrant-founded new ventures are more likely to go abroad sooner, they perform worse while their native counterparts take their time to plan and strategize and, therefore, although they are less likely to go abroad sooner, they perform better than immigrant-founded new ventures. For example, an immigrant entrepreneur conveys this overconfidence as follows:

> As an immigrant, I came with eight dollars in my pocket. The first thing you learn is, it's not about money. If you learn how to create something from nothing, how can you ever fail, because you can always make something from nothing. So once you learn how to make something from nothing, the world is your oyster.

Another explanation might be that the pressure for success for outsiders induces them to internationalize quickly. My field interviews suggest that outsider entrepreneurs feel obligated to be successful. Therefore, they want to start businesses that grow big quickly to show the world that they are successful. This pressure might cause outsider entrepreneurs to undertake growth strategies such as early internationalization prematurely, without careful analysis. On the other hand, not facing this kind of pressure for success, insider entrepreneurs, might undertake early internationalization only when it is the right strategy. A native entrepreneur explains this pressure that his immigrant co-founder faces:

> ...People from other countries that are coming here to become entrepreneurs, a lot of them are entrepreneurs, too. A lot of them have started their businesses. They run a circle where there is some competition, too. I think that's different than me as an entrepreneur here. I don't know that we have as much of that pressure to succeed. They put it on themselves. I think it starts with the goals. If you create these goals and you fixate on the goals, then there is that pressure that comes with it. I think for me living here I was more under the situation of, I'm going to give this a try. I kind of hope it works; if not, I can go get another a job. It was never, this is my only avenue to success.

Both "overconfidence" and "pressure for success" explanations are only anecdotal, and further empirical testing and validation is needed to substantiate these explanations.

As the last step, I compared several characteristics of immigrant versus native-founded *international* new ventures. Table 18 presents results from the t-tests on these differences on some of the key dimensions. Immigrant founders of international new ventures tend to be younger, more educated and have less previous work experience than native founders of international new ventures. In addition, international new ventures with immigrant founders are more likely to get VC financing and to be located in high-tech centers and in states with higher export intensity.

Discussion of Findings

Table 18: Comparison of the Means of Key Variables for Immigrant vs. Native-Founded International New Ventures

VARIABLE	Immigrant-Founded	Native-Founded	t-statistics	p-value
Gender	0.869 (0.072)	0.889 (0.291)	0.264	0.792
Age	44.434 (1.838)	48.949 (0.931)	2.003	0.047**
Education	8.652 (0.318)	6.750 (0.173)	-4.583	0.000***
Previous Work Exp.	12.609 (1.799)	17.342 (1.133)	1.766	0.079*
Previous Startup Exp.	1.652 (0.415)	1.453 (0.202)	-0.404	0.687
Internet Sales	0.391 (0.104)	0.479 (0.046)	0.764	0.446
Intellectual Property	0.478 (0.106)	0.427 (0.046)	-0.447	0.655
R&D Focus	0.319 (0.088)	0.262 (0.040)	-0.578	0.565
Sales Focus	0.398 (0.073)	0.618 (0.301)	0.326	0.745
VC Funded	0.235 (0.106)	0.032 (0.018)	-3.276	0.001**
Resource Mobility	0.795 (0.060)	0.726 (0.023)	-1.026	0.307
Total Assets ($)	12.109 (0.423)	12.381 (0.173)	0.616	0.539
High-Tech Center	0.681 (0.102)	0.351 (0.046)	-2.956	0.004**
State Export Intensity	7.305 (1.009)	4.648 (0.412)	-2.544	0.012**

*p <0.10, **p<0.05 (standard deviations are in parentheses), two-tailed test.

My observations from my qualitative analysis together with my quantitative findings seems to suggest that because of the higher pressure for success and overconfidence, immigrant entrepreneurs tend to start ventures with greater growth potential relative to native entrepreneurs. Because greater growth potential is often go together with greater risks, the nature of the business (i.e., high risk-high return) might be the reason for the higher failure rates for immigrant-founded international new ventures relative to native counterparts. Also, findings suggest that immigrant founders tend to have greater previous start up experiences although this difference is not significant. Finally, there is no difference between immigrant and native-founded international new ventures in terms of their total assets, resource mobility, intellectual property, internet sales, or their focus on R&D or sales activities. It is also important to note that the variance within the immigrant group is larger than the variance within the native group for each of the variables.

CHAPTER 9
Conclusion: Contributions, Limitations and Future Research Directions

This study makes several contributions to theory, methods and practice. The theoretical contributions include new insights into the concept of *"outsiderness"* and its role in the early internationalization and performance of new ventures. Specifically, this study examined the impact of founders' outsider status on early internationalization and the impact of founders' outsider status on firm survival and growth as moderated by early internationalization. Methodologically, this study is one of the first empirical studies to use a large longitudinal dataset to examine new venture strategies and performance. This study is also relevant and important not only for potential entrepreneurs in deciding their international strategies, but also for policy makers who aim to increase the competitiveness of the U.S. economy in today's global world. I will discuss these contributions in more detail below.

Theoretical Contributions
Building on the insights provided by the behavioral theory of the firm, this study has aimed to get a better understanding about the causes and consequences of new venture internationalization. In doing so, it contributes to literatures on international and immigrant entrepreneurship and strategic management literatures.

International Entrepreneurship:

One of the key contributions of this research is the finding that founders' immigrant status has a significantly positive effect on new venture internationalization. This finding contributes to the current state of the literature in international entrepreneurship. Although this literature has given considerable attention to the characteristics of founders as the main driver of new venture internationalization (Freeman & Cavusgil, 2007), it has not considered founders' country of origin as an important factor in explaining why some high-tech firms choose to internationalize early while others remain domestic-only, even though foreign born entrepreneurs play increasingly significant roles in high technology entrepreneurship (Hart et. al., 2009).

The findings emphasize the importance of founders' experiences with cross border mobility and their degree of social embeddeness in their local environment in shaping their international strategies. Moreover, the study examines many variables, for which the effects on early internationalization have been either unknown or inconclusive in the literature. For example, the study reported that founders' formal education, VC financing, and the mobility of firm resources have positive and significant effects on early internationalization.

Furthermore, there are very few empirical studies in the existing literature that test the effect of early internationalization on firm performance. Moreover, the results of the existing studies are mixed and inconclusive. For example, while some of studies found a negative relationship between early internationalization and firm survival (Fernhaber & McDougall-Covin, 2011), others find either no relationship (Mudambi & Zahra, 2007) or inconclusive findings (Carr, Haggard, Hmieleski & Zahra, 2010). For example, Bloodgood, Sapienza & Almedia (1996) found a positive relationship between early internationalization and income although they found no relationship between early internationalization and sales growth. In contrast, Carr, Haggard, Hmieleski & Zahra (2010) demonstrated a positive relationship between early internationalization and sales growth. By examining firm survival and firm growth in the same study, this study provides insights into the complicated nature of new venture performance and presents results that test the idea that early internationalization enhances the growth of those new ventures that are able to overcome deadly obstacles in foreign markets.

<u>Immigrant Entrepreneurship:</u>
This study contributes to immigrant entrepreneurship literature by providing a new insight into the concept of outsiderness. First, while most research in immigrant entrepreneurship literature has emphasized the disadvantages that outsider entrepreneurs face in their adopted country due to institutional pressures external to immigrant entrepreneurs, this study contributes to this literature by shedding light onto the cognitive aspects of outsiderness. Having early life experiences with personal mobility and lacking strong roots in their adopted county, immigrant entrepreneurs are free from the "local" mindsets and social obligations created by local social networks, and therefore they can act more freely and flexibly to take advantage of a broader set of opportunities both within and outside of their adopted countries. In line with this argument, the results provide evidence for the pursuit of a wider geographic scope by outsider founded new ventures relative to insider founded new ventures. One important implication is that *"outsiderness"* or foreignness is a two-edged sword; on one hand, it has largely been assumed that outsiderness is a liability limiting access to local resources, yet on the other hand, this study shows that it is also an asset that provides new ventures with more freedom, openness and flexibility for a broader market scope. Research in international studies has begun to examine the paradox of foreignness (Edman, 2009), and this research adds to this recent effort.

Second, the aforementioned disadvantages and advantages of outsiderness provide insights into the performance of insider versus outsider founded new ventures. The existing body of empirical studies in this literature focuses mainly on the performance of domestic-only new ventures founded by insider and outsider entrepreneurs. A sole examination of domestic-only ventures may not capture the entirety of differences between outsider and insider founded new venture performance, and therefore confines the identification of the true impact of founders' immigrant status on firm performance. This study found that independent of the international strategies of new ventures, there is no main effect of founders' outsider status on firm performance. This finding not only demonstrates that outsider status is not a sole advantage or disadvantage in and of itself, but also indicates that it is important to consider firm strategy in this relationship. Moreover, given the surprising result that outsider founded international new ventures have a lower rate of survival and growth relative to insider founded international new ventures, more research is needed to understand the dynamics of success for insider and outsider founded new ventures. This study therefore calls for a more comprehensive examination of the impact of outsiderness on firm performance.

Strategic Management:
This study also contributes to the strategic management literature. Almost no research exists in this literature that examines new venture strategies as a function of founders' country of origin, and the role of strategy as a moderator in the relationship between founders' country of origin and new venture performance. Strategies represent important means by which new ventures align their strength and weaknesses with the opportunities and threats in the environment (Porter, 1980). Given that entrepreneurs are the main strategy makers in new ventures, their characteristics in terms of their prior life experiences have direct implications for their strategic choices. Therefore, understanding how founders' countries of origin influence their strategic decisions is crucial to increase our understanding of why new ventures have divergent strategic choices and, hence, divergent performance outcomes.

This study found significant links between founders' immigrant status, early internationalization and new venture performance. Relationships between founder characteristics, firm strategy and performance are more direct and especially important in the context of high-tech new ventures. High-tech new ventures operate in an uncertain environment and suffer from limited resource availability or "liabilities of newness". In such a context, a bad decision by a founder might be hard to overcome and can easily cause the overall failure of the venture and vice versa. The findings of this study contribute to our understanding of how founders' country of origin plays a role in new ventures' market growth strategies and performance in high technology

Conclusion

industries. In particular, both the quantitative and the qualitative findings of this study show that immigrant status has a large influence on the internationalization path followed very early on in a new venture's life. While native entrepreneurs might perceive national and even state borders as barriers, immigrant entrepreneurs see them as opportunities to be exploited. In addition, results show that this perception of immigrant founders does not necessarily leads to better performance; in fact, their ventures do worse than those with native founders. This study, therefore, contributes to strategic management literature by providing important insights and surprising results about the relationships between founders' characteristics, strategy and performance.

Methodological Contributions

There are several methodological contributions of this study. First, this study uses the Kauffman Firm Survey, a data set of a cohort of large number of new businesses that all started in 2004 in the U.S. Because all new ventures in the data set are started in the same year and the same country, the unwanted variance due to starting in different years or in different institutional contexts is naturally eliminated in this dataset. Second, KFS is a longitudinal data set that is arguably the largest longitudinal dataset of new small businesses currently available. Examining a large number of new ventures over time helps address the issue of reverse causation. It also permits one to follow both successful firms as well as the failed ones in future years, which helps address the problem of survivor bias. Finally, the dataset includes comprehensive information about these firms, allows one to control for sources of variance other than the variables of interest in this study. Given that most of the existing quantitative work examining new ventures uses a small number of firms from different cohorts, cross sectional design, very limited number of controls, and suffers from reverse causation and survivor bias, this study is advancement in the quantitative empirical examination of new ventures.

Moreover, this study combines quantitative work with qualitative field interviews. A shortcoming of quantitative research is that, although it allows documenting statistical associations between variables, it cannot definitively explain the mechanism behind these associations. That level of detail can be gained only through qualitative analyses. Qualitative research, on the other hand, allows getting an in-depth understanding about the phenomena and the relationships, however, it cannot provide generalizable results. This study contributes to the literature by combining these two techniques and it benefits from the merits of these two types of research while minimizing their shortcomings.

Practical Contributions
This book has also practical importance. International new ventures now account for nearly 25 % of high technology new ventures (OECD,1997) and contribute innovation, job creation, and eventually contribute to the development and growth of their countries at rates higher than entrepreneurial firms in general (Hessels & Stel, 2007). Therefore, it is important both for potential entrepreneurs and policy makers to obtain a better understanding about the determinants and consequences of internationalization strategy.

This book provides a better understanding about who are more likely to become international entrepreneurs and how their ventures perform when they are domestic-only versus international. The results revealed that outsider entrepreneurs are more likely to start international new ventures but their ventures do not necessarily perform better than those new ventures founded by insider entrepreneurs. Based on this finding outsider and insider entrepreneurs might gain a better insight into how to go about early internationalization strategy including the differential forces that motivate or discourage their crossing borders very early on. Specifically, for outsider entrepreneurs, findings suggest that their global mind sets and lack of embeddedness encourage them to quickly internationalize, but findings also suggest that it might be a premature strategy and it may be important for outsider entrepreneurs to take more time and plan more before venturing abroad. For, insider entrepreneurs, findings suggest that their domestic mindsets and ties to local social context may it difficult for them to look outside for opportunities. This suggests that insider entrepreneurs should be aware of these forces and they should try to overcome them or maybe team up with immigrant entrepreneurs.

Conclusion

In addition, early internationalization is a risky strategy whoever the founder is. Results suggest that even though firms grow substantially when they become international, it is also true that many new ventures fail before they could reap the benefits because of the risks early internationalization also entails. Therefore, it is important for potential entrepreneurs to be aware of the costs and benefits of early internationalization upfront and decide if it is a right strategy for them. This would help them to avoid costly mistakes afterwards.

The findings have also important implications for policy makers. Given that, the competitiveness of the U.S. firms depends on their ability to tap international markets (Hart et al., 2009), these results may have implications for devising training and export stimulation programs targeting immigrant and native-founded high technology ventures to encourage international efforts by these firms. Moreover, policy makers might start various initiatives to address the impediments to the success of immigrant and native-founded new ventures face in international markets, and these initiatives might also include financial institutions including export credit agencies, export promotion agencies and other stakeholders to consider their respective roles in supporting the success of high technology new ventures in international markets.

Last but not the least, this study has an implication for the immigration policy. Immigrant-founded new ventures now account for 25.3% of all high-tech companies started in the US from 1995 to 2005. These companies produced $52 billion in sales and employed 450,000 workers in 2005 in the US (Wadhwa et al., 2007). Moreover, according to a recent survey by the National Venture Capital Association, immigrant entrepreneurs founded 25% of the ventured-backed companies that started in the last 15 years. The current market value of these companies exceeds $500 billion, and they employ 220,000 people in the U.S. and 400,000 people internationally (Klein, 2007).

Acknowledging the importance of highly skilled immigrant entrepreneurs for the U.S. economy, President Barak Obama (The New York Times, April 21, 2011) has stated that *"We want more Andy Groves [8] here in the United States. We don't want them starting Intel in China or starting it in France. We want them starting it here."* The

---

[8] A successful Hungarian-born immigrant entrepreneur who co-founded Intel.

findings of this study demonstrate that highly skilled immigrant entrepreneurs are highly mobile individuals who are inclined to pursue opportunities wherever they might be in the world. Therefore, policy makers should devise immigration policies to encourage highly skilled immigrants to come and start new businesses in the U.S. and in other developed countries around the world.

Limitations and Future Research Directions
Both the limitations and the findings of the study present avenues for future research. First, the data for this study come from high-tech new ventures that are started in the US. It is important to note that the U.S. provides a more stringent context to test the hypotheses of this study because it is a country known as *"the country of immigrants"*, which is especially more receptive of highly skilled immigrant entrepreneurs. Therefore, I expect that findings should hold even more strongly in other countries where the distinction between immigrant and native entrepreneurs are more salient. However, more research in other countries is needed to confirm the results of this study.

Second, this research does not examine the country selection choices. However, in order to get a better understanding of the early internationalization by immigrant versus native-founded firms, it is important to examine which countries that they enter, and the physic distance across these countries. Are native and immigrant entrepreneurs systematically differ in their country choices? My field interviews indicate that new ventures with native founders are attracted to countries with strong institutions. Then, the questions arise: Does this observation hold in larger samples? Are there differences between outsider and insider founded new ventures in the selection of countries? What are the performance implications of these decisions?

Third, this study measures early internationalization as having international sales and does not examine the mode of entry. Although in their seminal paper, Oviatt & McDougall (1994) argue that *"new ventures do not necessarily own foreign assets; in other words, foreign direct investment is not a requirement for early international entry,"* mode of entry is an important dimension to distinguish different approaches to early internationalization and entry mode and ownership corresponds well with the research in international business on the foreign direct investments of firms and allows us to compare internationalizing firms within and across age groups more easily. So, future research should examine entry mode decisions of immigrant and native-founded new ventures.

Fourth, this study makes no differentiation between immigrant entrepreneurs' home countries, the number of years that they have spent in the U.S. or whether they have got their latest training in the US or not. Because these characteristics might create significant variances within the group of immigrant entrepreneurs, future research should examine the implications of these differences for new venture strategy and performance. How do highly skilled immigrant entrepreneurs vary in their personal network structures in their adopted country? How does this variance affect early internationalization and performance of their ventures?

Finally, this study does not delve into founding team dynamics. Given that new ventures are increasingly founded by team of entrepreneurs especially in high technology industries, examining the team composition is a fruitful future research direction: is it the presence of an immigrant entrepreneur in the founding team that matters or is it necessary that all founding team members be immigrants to get the effect of outsiderness? Such theoretical specificity could enrich the discussion of the merits and demerits of having foreign founders for early internationalization and firm performance.

Conclusions

I set out to understand more fully the effects on a new venture of its having a native (insider) versus immigrant (outsider) founder. In particular, I wanted to shed light on the effects of founders on early internationalization strategy and performance. Drawing on the behavioral theory of the firm, I argued that because "outsider" entrepreneurs are more likely to possess global mindsets and less likely to have strong roots in their countries of adoption, they are more likely to build ventures that are international at or near their founding than are "insider" entrepreneurs, who are more likely to be subject to domestic mindsets and strong local ties. Moreover, I argued that the outsiders have some disadvantages in their adoptive country setting but some advantages if or when their new ventures go abroad. I predicted that outsiders are more likely to internationalize early than insiders, that early internationalizing firms have greater mortality but faster growth (if they survive) than domestic firms, and that among early internationalized firms those with immigrant founders do better in terms of survival and growth.

I found empirical support for the hypothesis that new ventures with immigrant founders are more likely to internationalize early. At the same time, I found evidence that early internationalization as a strategy has a negative effect on firm survival but I found no evidence that early internationalization has a significant effect on firm growth. Surprisingly, I found that immigrant-founded international ventures have greater mortality and lower growth than native-founded international new ventures. Supplementary analyses also showed that immigrant-founded *international* new ventures are less likely to survive and grow than immigrant-founded *domestic-only* new ventures.

That is, outsiderness in terms of having an immigrant founder opens up new horizons to the new venture, and drives early internationalization although it does not lead to better performance, with new international ventures with immigrant entrepreneurs not performing as well as those with native-born entrepreneurs. My qualitative data suggest that immigrant entrepreneurs tend to be overconfident in their own ability to internationalize successfully. Thus, this study inspires future research to understand the dynamics of success for insider and outsider entrepreneurs and their ventures.

The findings have also important implications for policy makers. Given that the competitiveness of U.S. firms depends on their ability to tap international markets (Hart et al., 2009), these results have implications for devising training and export stimulus programs targeting immigrant and native-founded high-tech ventures. Moreover, policy makers concerned with immigration policies for highly skilled immigrant entrepreneurs can also benefit from my results.

Appendix A

The List of High-Tech Centers in the U.S.

1. Automation Alley - Metropolitan Detroit (primarily Oakland County, Michigan)
2. Brainpower Triangle - Cambridge, Massachusetts, Somerville, Massachusetts
3. Cummings Research Park - Huntsville, Alabama
4. Denver Tech Center - Denver, Colorado
5. Dulles Technology Corridor - Northern Virginia near Washington Dulles Airport
6. Florida High Tech Corridor - Central Florida
7. Eastside - Puget Sound
8. Golden Corridor - Near Chicago's O'Hare International Airport and Northwest Suburbs
9. Illinois Technology and Research Corridor - DuPage County, Illinois
10. Optics Valley - Tucson, Arizona
11. Research Triangle - North Carolina
12. Route 128 - Massachusetts
13. Silicon Alley - New York City
14. Silicon Hills - Austin, Texas and its suburbs
15. Silicon Forest - Portland, Oregon
16. Silicon Prairie - Metropolitan Dallas (primarily the northern region and its suburbs)
17. Silicon Suburb - Cleveland, Ohio
18. Silicon Valley - Northern California
19. Tech Coast - Southern California
20. Tech Valley - The Capital District area of Albany, NY

21. Telecom Corridor (an area in the Silicon Prairie) - Richardson, suburb of Dallas, Texas
22. Texas Medical Center - Houston, Texas

Appendix B

SUBSAMPLE ANALYSES IN TESTING HYPOTHESIS 3a

Table B.1 Test of H3a (Subs-sample analysis): Probit Estimate of Firm Survival for International New Ventures

Estimators→ Variables ↓	β	St. Dev	z	p>|z|
Immigrant Status	**-1.277****	**0.495**	**-2.58**	**0.010**
Education	0.283***	0.105	2.70	0.007
Prev. Industry Experience	-0.004	0.014	-0.33	0.745
Prev. Startup Exp.	-0.035	0.056	-0.63	0.527
Intellectual Property	-0.802*	0.431	-1.86	0.063
Log (Tot. Assets $)	0.220***	0.082	2.67	0.008
Tech Generator Industry	-0.759	0.472	-1.61	0.108
Past Performance	-0.099	0.067	-1.49	0.136
High -Tech Center	0.133	0.379	0.35	0.726
Constant (α)	-2.149**	1.021	-2.10	0.035
Log Likelihood	-28.419			
N	131			

MfxDy/dx= -0.21 sd=0.12 z=-1.77 p=0.076

Table B.2. Test of H3a (Subs-sample analysis): Probit Estimate of Firm Survival for Domestic-Only New Ventures

Estimators→ Variables ↓	β	St. Dev.	z	p>|z|
Immigrant Status	**0.335**	**0.535**	**0.63**	**0.531**
Education	0.312***	0.087	3.56	0.000
Prev. Industry Experience	0.008	0.012	0.68	0.498
Prev. Startup Experience	-0.113*	0.069	-1.65	0.099
Intellectual Property	-0.164	0.362	-0.45	0.651
Log (Tot. Assets $)	0.122**	0.058	2.09	0.037
Tech Generator Industry	-0.547	0.347	-1.57	0.115
Past Performance (ROA_3)	0.009	0.027	0.37	0.711
High-Tech Center	0.461	0.306	1.51	0.132
Constant (α)	-1.550*	0.800	-1.94	0.053
Log Likelihood	-47.174			
N	220			

Mfx dy/dx= 0.021 sd=0.027 z=0.79 p=0.432

Appendix B

Table B.3 Test of H3a (Subs-sample analysis): Probit Estimate of Firm Survival for Immigrant-Founded New Ventures[1]

Estimators→ Variables ↓	β	St. Dev.	z	p>|z|
Early International	-8.335**	3.601	-2.31	0.021
Education	2.354**	1.040	2.26	0.024
Prev. Industry Experience	-0.067	0.058	-1.17	0.243
Prev. Startup Experience	1.113**	0.494	2.25	0.024
Log (Tot. Assets $)	-1.020*	0.542	-1.88	0.060
Past Performance (ROA_3)	0.825**	0.387	2.13	0.033
High -Tech Center	2.090	1.283	1.63	0.103
Constant (α)	4.611	3.730	1.24	0.216
Log Likelihood	-3.879			
N	39			

Mfx dy/dx= -0.000498   sd=0.0024   z=-0.21   p=0.835

[1] STATA drops intellectual property and technology generating industries variables from the analyses due to insufficient variance in these variables for immigrant-founded new ventures.

Table B.4 Test of H3a (Subs-sample analysis): Probit Estimate of Firm Survival for Native-Founded New Ventures[1]

Estimators→ Variables ↓	β	St. Dev.	z	p>|z|
Early International	**0.016**	**0.276**	**0.06**	**0.954**
Education	0.217***	0.067	3.26	0.001
Prev. Industry Experience	0.000	0.011	0.06	0.954
Prev. Startup Experience	-0.131**	0.052	-2.53	0.011
Log (Tot. Assets $)	0.116**	0.052	2.23	0.026
Past Performance (ROA_3)	-0.005	0.026	-0.18	0.854
High -Tech Center	0.292	0.271	1.08	0.281
Constant (α)	-0.976	0.695	-1.40	0.161
Log Likelihood	-62.022			
N	293			

Mfx dy/dx= 0.00143   sd=0.025   z=0.06   p=0.953

[1] Intellectual property and technology generating industries variables are dropped from the analyses to ensure consistency across two subsamples-immigrant and native-founded new ventures.

Appendix C

SUBSAMPLE ANALYSES IN TESTING HYPOTHESIS 3b

Table C.1 Test of H3b (Subs-sample analysis): Ordinary Least Square (OLS) Estimate of Firm Growth for International New Ventures

Estimators → Variables ↓	β	St. Deviation	t	p>|t|
Immigrant Status	-1.841	1.189	-1.55	0.126
Male	1.344	2.115	0.64	0.527
Education	-0.495	0.369	-1.34	0.183
Prev. Industry Exp.	-0.038	0.046	-0.82	0.414
Prev. Startup Exp.	0.082	0.180	0.46	0.648
Internet Sales	0.335	0.858	0.39	0.697
Intellectual Property	2.339	1.710	1.37	0.175
Log (Tot. Assets_2 $)	0.632	0.550	1.15	0.254
VC Funded	3.869*	1.974	1.96	0.054
Tech Gen Industry	1.045	0.954	1.10	0.277
R&D Focus	-4.118	3.367	-1.22	0.225
Sales Focus	1.819	2.090	0.87	0.387
Log (Sales_2 $)	-1.966*	1.128	-1.74	0.085
High -Tech Center	-0.712	1.067	-0.67	0.507
Constant (α)	21.436**	10.732	2.00	0.049
F Statistics	0.61			
R2	0.25			
N	92			

Mfx dy/dx= -1.840 sd=1.189 z=-1.55 p=0.122

Table C.2 Test of H3b (Subs-sample analysis): Ordinary Least Square (OLS) Estimate of Firm Growth for Domestic-Only New Ventures

Estimators→ Variables ↓	β	St. Deviation	t	p>|t|
Immigrant Status	**1.842**	**1.551**	**1.19**	**0.237**
Male	1.176	0.853	1.38	0.171
Education	0.299	0.220	1.36	0.177
Prev. Industry Experience	-0.045	0.035	-1.26	0.209
Prev. Startup Experience	0.248	0.245	1.01	0.313
Internet Sales	0.663	1.004	0.66	0.510
Intellectual Property	0.068	1.066	0.06	0.949
Log (Tot. Assets_2 $)	0.521*	0.289	1.80	0.074
VC Funded	1.385	3.539	0.39	0.696
Tech Generator Industry	-0.753	0.727	-1.03	0.303
R&D Focus	1.447	1.259	1.15	0.253
Sales Focus	-1.892**	0.847	-2.23	0.027
Log (Sales_2 $)	-1.292**	0.577	-2.24	0.027
High -Tech Center	-0.199	0.406	-0.49	0.624
Constant (α)	8.707**	4.211	2.07	0.041
F Statistics	0.88			
R2	0.261			
N	129			

Mfx dy/dx=1.842 sd=1.55 z=1.19 p=0.235

Table C.3 Test of H3b (Subs-sample analysis): Ordinary Least Square (OLS) Estimate of Firm Growth for Immigrant- Founded Ventures

Estimators→ Variables ↓	β	St. Deviation	t	p>|t|
Early International	-4.626**	1.813	-2.55	0.043
Male	0.672	3.815	0.18	0.866
Education	0.364	0.694	0.52	0.619
Prev. Industry Experience	0.083	0.090	0.92	0.393
Prev. Startup Experience	1.715*	0.759	2.26	0.065
Internet Sales	1.384	1.923	0.72	0.499
Intellectual Property	-0.232	2.425	-0.10	0.927
Log (Tot. Assets_2 $)	1.992**	0.779	2.56	0.043
VC Funded	0.615	3.246	0.19	0.856
Tech Generator Industry	-2.193	1.663	-1.32	0.235
R&D Focus	-0.029	0.919	-0.03	0.976
Sales Focus	-3.586**	0.999	-3.59	0.012
Log (Sales_2 $)	-3.828***	0.765	-5.00	0.002
High -Tech Center	-5.041***	1.196	-4.21	0.006
Constant (α)	24.872*	10.731	2.32	0.060
F Statistics				
R^2				
N	21			

Mfx dy/dx= -4.626 sd=1.813 z=-2.55 p=0.011

Table C.4 Test of H3b (Subs-sample analysis): Ordinary Least Square (OLS) Estimate of Firm Growth for Native-Founded Ventures

Estimators → Variables ↓	Coefficient	St. Deviation	t	p>|t|
Early International	**0.629**	**0.778**	**0.81**	**0.420**
Male	0.648	0.758	0.85	0.394
Education	-0.023	0.188	-0.12	0.903
Prev. Industry Experience	-0.025	0.028	-0.86	0.389
Prev. Startup Experience	0.063	0.140	0.45	0.655
Internet Sales	0.725	0.700	1.04	0.302
Intellectual Property	1.246	1.014	1.23	0.221
Log (Tot. Assets_2 $)	0.645*	0.328	1.96	0.051
VC Funded	4.211	2.696	1.56	0.120
Tech Generator Industry	-0.331	0.576	-0.58	0.566
R&D Focus	-0.373	1.799	-0.21	0.836
Sales Focus	-0.389	1.427	-0.27	0.785
Log (Sales_2 $)	-1.475**	0.614	-2.40	0.017
High -Tech Center	-0.277	0.466	-0.59	0.553
Constant (α)	11.420**	4.813	2.37	0.019
F Statistics	1.00			
R^2	0.159			
N	200			

Mfx dy/dx= 0.629 sd=0.778 z=0.81 p=0.419

Appendix D

THE INTERVIEW PROTOCOL

Personal Questions:
1. Where are you originally from?
2. How long have you been in the US?
3. What is your immigration status?
4. What was the original reason for which you came to the US?
5. What is your most advanced degree? Which school?

Firm Specific Questions:
6. What is your company doing?
   What is your product or service?
7. What is the composition of the entrepreneurial team? (How many people? How many of them are immigrants? Same country?)
8. What motivated you to start a company in the US?
   What were the main difficulties during the process?
   What helped you most during the process?
   How did the fact that you (or the team members) are an immigrant (immigrants) play a role in this process?
9. Where did you get your financing from? What sources? How much?
   What were the main difficulties in getting financing?
   What helped you most to get financing?
10. How difficult would it be to switch your assets, move them to different locations and uses?

11. Do you consciously think about how much you put in fixed assets and more liquid assets?

International Strategy Questions:
12. Is your company international and in what ways?
    If not, then, Are you planning to? Why? When? Which countries?
    If yes, then, Why did you internationalize? And when? Which countries did you enter and why? How did the fact that you are an immigrant play a role in this process?
13. What are the advantages and disadvantages of being an international company?

Performance Questions:
14. Do you consider your company successful? Why?
15. What do you attribute the success/not success of your business?
16. As the founder what role did you play in this success? How did you contribute to this success/not success?
17. Do your international operations contribute to this success? Why? / Why not?

Is there anything you would like to add?

Appendix E

Testing the Effect of Immigrant Status on Geographic Market Scope of Domestic-Only New Ventures

To test the effect of immigrant status on the geographic market scope of domestic-only new ventures, I first operationalize *Domestic Geographic Market Scope,* a categorical variable to the following question asked in year 3 (2007): "Please indicate the place where the most of your customers are located." It is coded as 1= In neighborhoods local to business, 2= In the same city or county, 3= In the same state, 4= Nationwide. For the empirical analysis, category 1 and 2 is merged in order to make each category more distinct in representing a firm's geographic market scope and increasing the sample size in each category. This operationalization measures the extent to which a new venture targets markets outside its local market, and it is consistent with prior literature (McCann, 1991).

Multinomial logistic regression is used for the analysis because the dependent variable-domestic geographic market scope- consists of more than two categories. The first category is chosen as the comparison category, or the base case, meaning that separate relative risk ratios are determined for all independent variables for each category of the dependent variable with the exception of the comparison category. The results in Table A4 show that *founder immigrant status* is positively and significantly associated with statewide geographic market scope relative to the comparison category -local neighborhood- with z=18.25, p<0.000 for statewide, z=15.373, p<0.000 for nationwide. This result provides support to eliminate the alternative explanation that early internationalization of immigrant-founded new ventures is driven by home country pull effect.

Table E.1 Multi-nominal Logit Estimate of Domestic Geographic Market Scope[1]

Base Outcome, Neighborhood (1)

Estimators→ Variables ↓	β	St. Deviation	z	p>|z|
Statewide (2)				
Immigrant Status	15.587***	0.854	18.25	0.000
Male	-0.442	0.603	-0.73	0.463
Age	0.046**	0.023	1.99	0.047
Education	-0.184	0.129	-1.42	0.156
Prev. Industry Experience	0.010	0.029	0.35	0.727
Prev. Startup Experience	0.018	0.184	0.10	0.922
Providing Product	0.494	0.549	0.90	0.368
Internet Sales	-0.057	0.621	-0.09	0.927
Intellectual Property	1.049	0.684	1.53	0.125
R&D Focus	0.1667	0.714	0.23	0.815
Sales Focus	-0.400	0.591	-0.68	0.497
Resource Mobility	0.139	0.564	0.26	0.799
Log(Total Assets $)	0.346**	0.135	2.57	0.010
Past Performance (ROA_2)	0.850***	0.251	3.39	0.001
Tech Generator Industry	0.628	0.779	0.81	0.420
High-Tech Center	0.995	0.623	1.60	0.110
Metropolis or not	0.214	0.519	0.41	0.680
Constant (α)	-0.266**	2.060	-2.56	0.011

[1] This analysis is conducted on domestic-only new ventures.

Appendix E

Table E.1 Multi-nominal Logit Estimate of Domestic Geographic Market Scope (continued)

Estimators→ Variables ↓	Coefficient	St. Deviation	z	p>|z|
Nationwide (3)				
Immigrant Status	15.373***	0.955	16.09	0.000
Male	0.448	0.693	0.65	0.518
Age	0.027	0.025	1.11	0.267
Education	-0.157	0.139	-1.13	0.258
Prev. Industry Experience	0.001	0.032	0.04	0.968
Prev. Startup Experience	0.345*	0.180	1.92	0.055
Providing Product	0.843	0.681	1.24	0.216
Internet Sales	0.892	0.642	1.39	0.164
Intellectual Property	2.302***	0.737	3.12	0.002
R&D Focus	0.850	0.826	1.03	0.304
Sales Focus	-0.350	0.696	-0.50	0.615
Resource Mobility	-0.539	0.622	-0.87	0.387
Log(Tot. Assets $)	0.276*	0.166	1.67	0.095
Past Performance (ROA_2)	-0.052	0.122	-0.43	0.670
Tech Generator Industry	1.928**	0.825	2.34	0.019
High-Tech Center	0.324	0.748	0.43	0.665
Metropolis or not	-1.442**	0.649	-2.22	0.026
Constant (α)	-5.402**	2.487	-2.17	0.030
N = 161	Pseudo R2=0.2597		Log Likelihood= -126.6702	

References

Acs, Z.J., Morck, R., Shaver M., & Yeung, B. (1997). "The internationalization of small and medium sized enterprises: A policy perspective." *Small Business Economics*, 9(1):7-20.

Adler, P. & Kwon, S. (2002). "Social capital: Prospects for a new concept." *Academy of Management Review*, 27(1):17-40.

Agresti, A. (1996). *An Introduction to Categorical Data Analysis*. NY: John Wiley.

Aldrich, H E., & Fiol, MC. (1994). "Fools rush in? The institutional context of industry creation." *Academy of Management Review*, 19(4): 645-671.

Aldrich, H., & Waldinger, R. (1990). "Ethnicity and entrepreneurship." *Annual Review of Sociology*, (16):111-135.

Aldrich, H., Cater, J., Jones, T. & McEvoy, D. (1981). "Business development and self-Asian enterprise in three British cities." 170-90 In *Ethnic Segregation in Cities*, edited by Peach, C., Robinson, V and Smith, S. Croom Helm.

Almor, T., (2000). Born global: The case of small and medium sized, knowledge-intensive Israeli firms. In: Almor, T. and Hashai, N., Editors, 2000. *FDI, International Trade and the Economics of Peacemaking*, The College of Management, Academic Studies Division, Rishon LeZion, Israel.

Anderson, S., & Platzer, M. (2008). *American Made: the Impact of Immigrant Entrepreneurs and Professionals on U.S. Competitiveness*. Arlington, Virginia: National Venture Capital Association.

Andersson, S., Gabrielsson, J., & Wictor, I. (2004). "International activities in small firms: Examining factors influencing the internationalization and export growth of small firms." *Canadian Journal of Administrative Sciences*, 21(1): 22-34.

Angrist JD., & Pischke, J.S. (2009). *Mostly Harmless Econometrics*, Princeton University Press, New Jersey.

Arora, A., Jaju, A., Kefalas, A.G. & Perenich, T. (2004). "An exploratory analysis of global managerial mindsets: a case of US textile and apparel industry," *Journal of International Management*, 10(3): 393–411.

Aspelund, A., Madsen, T.K., Moen, O. (2007). "A review of the foundation, international marketing strategies, and performance of new ventures," *European Journal of Marketing*, 41(11/12): 1423-1448.

Autio, E., Sapienza, H., & Almeida, J. (2000). "Effects of age at entry, knowledge intensity, and imitability on international growth." *Academy of Management Journal*, 43(5):909-924.

Axinn, C. (1988). "Export performance: Do managerial perceptions make a difference?" *International Marketing Review* 5: 61-71.

Baron, RM., & Kenny, DA. (1986). "The moderator-mediator variable distinction in social psychological research: conceptual, strategic, and statistical considerations," *Journal of Personality and social Psychology*, 15(6):1173-1182.

Bates, T. (1997). "Financing small business creation: The case of Chinese and Korean immigrant entrepreneurs." *Journal of Business Venturing*, 12(2): 109-124.

Bell, J. (1995) "The internationalization of small computer software firms," *European Journal of Marketing* **29**(8): 60–75.

Berg, B.L. (1995). *Qualitative Research Methods for Social Sciences*, 3rd Edition. MA.

Bhide, A. (2008). *The Venturesome Economy.* Princeton University Press, New Jersey.

Bhide, A. (2000). *The Origin and Evolution of New Businesses*. Oxford University Press, New York, NY.

Bloodgood, J.M., Sapienza, HJ., & Almeida, JG. (1996). "The internationalization of new high-potential US ventures: Antecedents and outcomes," *Entrepreneurship Theory and Practice*, 20:61-76.

Bonte, W., Falck, O., Heblich, S. (2009). "The impact of regional age structure on entrepreneurship." *Economic Geography*, 67(3-4):687-698.

Bouquet, C.A. (2005). *Building Global Mindsets: An Attention-Based Perspective,* Palgrave Macmillan: New York.

Bromiley, P. (2005). *The Behavioral Foundations of Strategic Management Research*. Blackwell. USA.

References

Buckley, P. (2002). "Is the international business research agenda running out of steam?" *Journal of International Business Studies*, 33(2): 365-373.

Buckley, P., & Lessard, DR. (2005). "Regaining the edge for international business research." *Journal of International Business Studies*, 36(6):595-599.

Burgel, O., & Murray, G. (2000). "The international market choices of startup companies in high technology industries." *Journal of International Marketing*, 8(2):33-62.

Burpitt, W.J., Rondinelli, D.A. (2000). "Small firms' motivations for exporting: To earn and learn?" *Journal of Small Business Management*, 38(4), 1-14.

Klein, K (2007, March 19). "Immigrant Entrepreneurs," *Business Week*.

Cabrol, M., & Nlemvo, F. (2009). "The internationalization of French new ventures: The case of the Rhone-Alps region." *European Management Journal*, 27: 255–267.

Carpenter, M.A., Pollock, T.G. & Leary, M.M. (2003). "Testing a model of reasoned risk –taking: governance, the experience of principals and agents, and global strategy in high-technology IPO firms," *Strategic Management Journal*, 24(9):803-820.

Carr, J.C., Haggard, K.S., Hmieleski, K.M., Zahra, S.A. (2010). "A study of the moderating effects of firm age at internationalization on firm survival and short-term growth." *Strategic Entrepreneurship Journal*, 4(2):183-192.

Casillas, J.C., Moreno, A.M., Acedo, F.J., Gallego, M.A. (2009). "An integrative model of the role of knowledge in the internationalization process." *Journal of World Business*, 44(3), 311-322.

Casillas, J.C; Navarro, J.L. & Sapienza, 2010. Effects of knowledge acquisition and initial export activity on export intention." *Working Paper*.

Cavusgil, T & Knight, G. (2009). *Born Global firms*, Business Expert Press. USA.

Coviello, N., & Munro, H. (1995). "Growing the entrepreneurial firm." *European Journal of Marketing*, 49-61.

Chaganti, R. S., Watts, A. D., Chaganti, R., & Zimmerman-Treichel, M. (2008). "Ethnic-immigrants in founding teams: Effects on prospector strategy and performance in new Internet ventures." *Journal of Business Venturing*. 23(1): 113-139.

Chaganti, R., & Greene, PG. (2002). "Who are ethnic entrepreneurs? A study of entrepreneurs' ethnic involvement and business characteristics." *Journal of Small Business Management*, 40(2): 126-143.

Chandra, Y., Styles, C., & Wilkinson, I. (2009). "The recognition of first time international entrepreneurial opportunities: Evidence from firms in knowledge-based industries." *International Marketing Review*, 26(1): 30-61.

Chetty, S. & Campbell-Hunt, C. (2004). "A strategic approach to internationalization: a traditional versus 'born global' approach." *Journal of International Marketing*, 12(1): 57-81.

Chung, W & Alcácer, J. (2001) "Location Strategy for Agglomeration Economies", *Working Paper*.

Collins, J. & Low, A. (2010). "Asian female entrepreneurs in small and medium sized businesses in Australia." *Entrepreneurship & Regional Development*, 22(1): 97-111.

Coviello, N.E. (2006). "The network dynamics of international new ventures." *Journal of International Business Studies*, 37 (5): 713-728.

Coviello, N.E. & Munro, H. (1995). "Growing the entrepreneurial firm: Networking for international market development." *European Journal of Marketing*, 29(7): 49-61.

Crick, D. and M. V. J. (2000). "Small high technology firms and international high technology markets.", *Journal of International Marketing*, 8 (2): 63-85.

Crick, D. & Spence, M. (2005). "The internationalization of "high performing" UK high-tech SMEs: A study of planned and unplanned strategies." *International Business Review*, 14(2): 167-185.

Cyert, R. M. & March, J.G. (1963). *A Behavioral Theory of the Firm*, 2nd ed. Prentice Hall, Englewood Cliffs, NJ.

Dahlquist, J, P. Davidsson, P. & Wiklund, J. (2000). "Initial conditions as predictors of new venture performance: A replication and extension of the Cooper et al. study." *Enterprise and Innovation Management Studies*, 1 (1): 1-17.

Dana, L.P., Etemad, H. & Wright, R.W. (1999). "Theoretical foundations of international entrepreneurship." In: Rugman, AM & Wright, RW Ed., *Research in Global Strategic Management*. Vol.7. JAI Press, Stamford Conn (pp. 3-22).

References

Dana, L.P. (1997). "The origins of self-employment in ethno-cultural communities: distinguishing between orthodox entrepreneurship and reactionary enterprise." *Canadian Journal of Administrative Sciences*, 14: 52–68.

DeClerq, D., Sapienza, H., Yavuz, R.I. & Zhou, L. (2012). "Learning and Knowledge in International Entrepreneurship Research: Past Accomplishments and Future Directions." *Journal of Business Venturing*, 27(1), 143-165.

Dencker, J., Gruber, M. & Shah, S. (2009). "Pre-entry knowledge, learning, and the survival of new firms." *Organization Science.* 20(3): 516-537.

Eckhardt, J., Shane, S., & Delmar, F. (2006). "Multi-stage selection and the financing of new ventures." *Management Science*, 52(2): 220-232.

Eden, L & Miller, S. (2004). "Distance Matters: Liability of Foreignness, Institutional Distance and Ownership Strategy." In Hitt, M.A. & J.L.C. Cheng, editors, *Advances in International Management: The Evolving Theory of the Multinational Firm*. Amsterdman, Netherlands: Elsevier.

Edman, J. (2009). *Paradox of Foreignness,* Unpublished Dissertation.

Eriksson, K., Johanson, J., Majkga°rd, A., & Sharma, D. D. (1997). "Experiential knowledge and cost in the internationalization process." *Journal of International Business Studies,* 28(2), 337–360.

Eriksson, K., Majkgard, A., & Sharma, D. D. (2000). "Path dependence in the internationalization process." *Management International Review,* 40(4), 307–328.

Etemad, H. (2004). "International entrepreneurship as a dynamic adaptive system." *Journal of International Entrepreneurship,* 1:187-215.

Fairlie RW. (2008). "Estimating the contribution of immigrant business owners to the US economy." Santa Cruz: Small Business Administration, Office of Advocacy. http://archive.sba.gov/advo/research/rs334tot.pdf

Fairlie RW. & Meyer, B.D. (1996). "Ethnic and racial self-employment differences and possible explanations." *The Journal of Human Resources,* 31(4): 757-793.

Fan, T & Phan, P. (2007). "International new ventures: Revisiting the influences behind the 'born global' firm." *Journal of International Business Studies,* 38:1113-1131.

Fazzari, Hubbard & Petersen, (1988). "Financial constraints and corporate investment." *Brooking Papers on Economic Activity,* 1:141-206.

References

Federico, J.S., Kantis, H.D. Rialp, A. & Riapl, J. (2009). "Does entrepreneurs' human and relational capital affect early internationalization? A cross-regional comparison." *European Journal of International Management,* 3(2): 199-2105.

Fernhaber,S.A. & Li, D. (2010). "The impact of inter organizational imitation on new venture international entry and performance." *Entrepreneurship Theory & Practice,* 34(1): 1-30.

Fernhaber,S.A., McDougall-Covin, P.P. & Shepherd, D.A.(2009). "International entrepreneurship: Leveraging internal and external knowledge sources." *Strategic Entrepreneurship Journal,* 3(4):297-320.

Freeman, S., & Cavusgil, T. (2007). "Toward a typology of commitment states among managers of born-global firms: A study of accelerated internationalization." *Journal of International Marketing,* 1-40.

Gabrielsson, M., Kirpalani, V.H.M., Dimitratos. P., Solberg, A.A., Zucchella, A. (2008). "Born globals: Propositions to help advance the theory." *International Business Review,* 17(4): 385-401.

Gabrielsson, M. and Al-Obaidi, Z. (2004), "Pricing Strategies of Born Globals", in F. McDonald, M. Mayer,and T. Buck (eds.), *The Process of Internationalization,* New York: Palgrave Macmillan, 232–252.

Gassmann, O., & Keupp, M. M. (2007). "The competitive advantage of early and rapidly internationalising SMEs in the biotechnology industry: A knowledge based view." *Journal of World Business,* 42(3):350-366.

Goshal, S (1987). "Global strategy: An organizing framework." *Strategic Management Journal,* 8: 425-440.

Granovetter, M. (1995). "The economic sociology of firms and entrepreneurs. In A. Portes, *The Economic Sociology of Immigration* (pp. 128-165). New York: Russell Sage Foundation.

Gregoire, D., Williams, D.W., & Oviatt, B.M. (2008). "Early Internationalization decisions for new ventures: What matters?" Babson College Entrepreneurship Research Conference Paper.

Gudykunst, W.B. (1983). *Inter-cultural Communication Theory,* Sage Publications: Beverly Hills, CA.

Gulati R., Nohria, N., & Zaheer, A. (2000). "Strategic networks." *Strategic Management Journal,* 21(3):203-2015.

Gupta, AK., Govindarajan, V., & Wang H. (2008). *The Quest for Global Dominance.* Wiley Publishing: New Jersey.

References

Hadlock, P, Hecker, D. & Gannon, J. (1991). "High technology employment: another view." *Monthly Labor Review*, 26–30.

Harris s., & Wheeler, C. (2005). "Entrepreneurs' relationships for internationalization: Functions, origins and strategies." *International Business Review*, 14(2): 187-207.

Hart, D., Acs, Z., & Tracy, S. (2009). "High-tech Immigrant Entrepreneurship in the United States." Washington: Small Business Administration Office of Advocacy. http://archive.sba.gov/advo/research/rs349tot.pdf

Herman, RT., & Smith, RL. (2009). *Immigrant Inc. Why Immigrant Entrepreneurs are Driving the New Economy*. Wiley Publishing. New Jersey.

Hessels, J. (2008). International entrepreneurship: An introduction, framework, and research agenda." Business and Policy Research.

Hessels, J., & Stel, A. (2007). "Export orientation among new ventures and economic growth." ERIM Report Series Research in Management.

Hughes, M, Martin, S.L., Morgan, R.E., & Robson, M.J. (2010). "Realizing product-market advantage in high technology international new ventures: The mediating role of ambidextrous innovation." *Journal of International Marketing*, 18(4):1-21.

Hunt, J., & Gauthier-Loiselle, M. (2008). "How much does immigration boost innovation?" *NBER Working Papers*, 14312, National Bureau of Economic Research.

Hymer, S. H. (1976). *The International Operations of National Firms: A Study of Direct Investment*. Cambridge, Mass: The MIT Press.

Insch, G. & Miller, S. (2005). "Perception of Foreignness: Benefit or Liability?" *Journal of Managerial Issues*, 17(4): 423-38.

Iyer, G. & Shapiro, J. (1999). "Ethnic entrepreneurial and marketing systems: Implications for the global economy." *Journal of International Marketing*, 7(4):83-110.

Johanson, J., & Vahlne, J.E., (2009). The Uppsala internationalization process model revisited: from liability of foreignness to liability of outsidership. Journal of International Business Studies, 40, 1411-1431.

Johanson, J., & Vahlne, J. (1977). "The internationalization process of the firm - A model of knowledge development and increasing market commitment." *Journal of International Business Studies*, 8:23-32.

References

Jones, M. V. (1999). "The internationalization of small high technology firms." *Journal of International Marketing,* 7(4):15-41.

Kalnins, A., & Chung, W. (2006). "Social capital, geography, and survival: Gujarati immigrant entrepreneurs in the U.S. lodging industry." *Management Science,* 52(2): 233-247.

Kerr, W.R. (2008). "The ethnic composition of US investors." *Working Paper 08-006.*

Keupp, MM., Gassmann, O. (2009). "The past and the future of international entrepreneurship: A review and suggestions for developing the field." *Journal of Management,* 35(3):600-633.

Kirchhoff, B.A., Spencer, A. (2008). "New high technology firm contributions to economic growth," International Council for Small Business World Conference, Halifax, Canada.

Kirzner, I. (1997). "Entrepreneurial discovery and the competitive market process: An Austrian approach." *Journal of Economic Literature,* 35:60-85.

Knight, G., & Cavusgil, S. (2004). "Innovation organizational capabilities and the born global firm." *Journal of International Business Studies,* 35(2): 124-141.

Knight, G., & Cavusgil, S. (1996). "The born global firm: Achallenge to traditional internationalization theory." *Advances in International Marketing,* 8:11-26.

Kuemmerle, W. (2002). "Home base and knowledge management in international ventures," *Journal Business Venturing,* 17(2): 99-122.

Levitt, B.; & March, J. (1988). "Organizational learning." *Annual Review of Sociology,* 14:319-340.

Levy, O. (2005). "The influence of top management team attentional patterns on global strategic posture of firms." *Journal of Organizational Behavior,* 26(7): 797–819.

Levy, O., Beechler, S., Taylor, S. & Boyacigiller, N. (2007). "What we talk about when we talk about 'global mindset': Managerial cognition in multinational corporations." *Journal of International Business,* 38: 231-258.

Light, I. (1979). "Disadvantaged minorities in self-employment." *International Journal of Comparative Sociology,* 20:31-45.

References

Lofstorm, M. (2002). "Labor market assimilation and the self-employment decision of immigrant entrepreneurs." *Journal of Population Economics*, 15(1): 83-114.

Madsen, T.K, & Knudsen, T., (2003). "International new ventures: A new organizational form? *Conference Paper,"* The Sixth McGill Conference on International Entrepreneurship: Northern Ireland.

Madsen, T.K., Rasmussen, E.S. & Servais P. (2000). "Differences and similarities between Born Globals and other types of exporters." *Advances in International Marketing,* 10: 247-265.

Madsen, TK., & Servais, P. (1997). "The internationalization of born globals: An Evolutionary process?" *International Business Review,* 6(6): 561-583.

March, J.G. (1994). *A Primer on Decision Making.* Free Press: New York.

March, J.G, Simon, HA. (1958). *Organizations.* Wiley: New York.

Mathew, JA., & Zander, I. (2007). "The entrepreneurial dynamics of accelerated internationalization." *Journal of International Business Studies,* 38:387-403.

Maxwell, J.A. (1996). Qualitative Research Design: *An Interactive Approach.* Thousand Oaks, CA: Sage.

McDougall, P., Shane, S., & Oviatt, B. (1994). "Explaining the formation of international new ventures: The limits of international business research." *Journal of Business Venturing,* 9:469-487.

McCann, J. E. (1991)."Patterns of growth, competitive technology, and financial strategies in young ventures." *Journal of Business Venturing,* 6: 189-203.

McCracken, G. (1990). *The Long Interview.* Sage University Press: California.

McKinzey and Co. (1993). "Emerging exporters: Australia's high value-added manufacturing exporters." Melbourne: Australian Manufacturing Council.

Mezias, J. M. (2002). "Identifying liabilities of foreignness and strategies to minimize their effects: The case of labor lawsuit judgments in the United States." *Strategic Management Journal*, 23(3): 229-44.

Miller, S. & Richards, M. (2002). "Liability of foreignness and membership in a regional economic group: Analysis of the European Union." *Journal of International Management*, 8: 323.

Morris, M. & Schindehutte, M. (2005). "Entrepreneurial Values and the Ethnic Enterprise: An Examination of Six Subcultures." *Journal of Small Business Management*, 43(4): 453-479.
Mudambi, R., Zahra, S. A. (2007). "The survival of international new ventures." *Journal of International Business Studies* 38: 333-352.
Murphy, G.B., Trailer, J.W., & Hill, R.C. (1996). "Measuring performance in entrepreneurship research," *Journal of Business Research*, 36:15-23.
Muzychenko, O. (2008). "Cross-cultural entrepreneurial competence in identifying international business opportunities." *European Management Journal*, 26(6): 366-377.
Nordman, E.R. & Melen, S. (2008). The impact of different kinds of knowledge for the internationalization process of Born Globals in the biotech business, *Journal of World Business*, 43(2):171-185.
Nummela, N., Saarenketo, S., & Puumalainen, K. (2004). "Rapidly with a rifle or more slowly with a shotgun? Stretching the company boundaries of internationalizing ICT firms." *Journal of International Entrepreneurship*, 2(4):275-288.
OECD (1997). *Development Co-operation Report*. Paris http://www.oecd-ilibrary.org/development/development-co-operation-report-1997_dcr-1997-en
Orser, B., Riding, A., & Townsend, J. (2004). "Exporting as a means of growth for women-owned Canadian SMEs." *Journal of Small Business and Entrepreneurship*, 17(3):153-174.
Oviatt, B., & McDougall, P. (2005). "Defining International Entrepreneurship and Modeling the Speed of Internationalization." *Entrepreneurship Theory and Practice*, 537-553.
Oviatt, B., & McDougall, P. (1995). "Global start-ups: Entrepreneurs on a worldwide stage." *Academy of Management Executive*, 9(2):30-43.
Oviatt, B., & McDougall, P. (1994). "Toward a theory of international new ventures."*Journal of International Business Studies,* 25(1):45-64.
Packalen, K. (2007). "Complementing capital: The role of status, demographic features, and social capital in founding teams abilities to obtain resources." *Entrepreneurship Theory and Practice*, 31(6):873-891.
Pedersen, T. & Shaver, J.M. (2002). "Internationalization revisited: The 'big step' hypothesis," *Working Paper.*

References

Pieterse, J. N. (2006). "Social capital and migration - Beyond ethnic economies." In S. Radcliffe, *Culture and Development in a Globalizing World: Geographies, Actors, and Paradigms* (pp. 126-149). New York: Routledge Publishing.

Porter, M (1980). *Competitive Strategy*. Free Press, New York.

Portes, A., Guarnizo, L.E., Haller, W. (2002). "Transnational entrepreneurs: An alternative form of immigrant economic adaptation." *American Sociological Review*, 278-298.

Portes, A. (1995). *The Economic Sociology of Immigration*. New York: Russel Sage Foundation.

Preece, S.B., Miles, G. & Baetz, M.C. (1999). "Explaining the international intensity and global diversity of early-stage technology-based firms," *Journal of Business Venturing*, 14(3): 259-281.

Ram, M., Smallbone, D., Deakins, D. and Jones, T. (2003). "Banking on "break-out": Finance and the development of ethnic minority businesses", *Journal of Ethnic and Migration Studies*, 29(4): 663-81.

Rasmussen, E.S. & Madsen, T.K. (2002). "The born global concept." *Conference Paper*, the EIBA Conference.

Rasmussen, E.S. & Madsen, T.K. & Evangelista, F. (2001). "The founding of the born global company in Denmark and Australia: sense making and networking," *Asia Pacific Journal of Management*, 13(3): 75-107.

Rath, J. & R. Kloosterman .(2000) "Outsiders' business. Research of immigrant entrepreneurship in the Netherlands", *International Migration Review*, 34 (3): 656-680.

Reavley, M., Litchy, T., & McClelland, E. (2005). "Exporting success: A two country comparison of women entrepreneurs in international trade." *International Journal of Entrepreneurial and Small Business*. 2(1):57-78.

Rennie, M.(1993). Global competitiveness: Born global, *McKinsey Quarterly*, 4: 45–52.

Rialp A., Rialp, J., & Knight, GA. (2005). "The phenomenon of early internationalizing firms: What do we know after a decade (1993-2003) of scientific inquiry?" *International Business Review*, 14(2):147-166.

Robb, A., Ballou, J., DesRoches, D., Potter, F., Zhao, Z. & Reedy, E.J. (2009). "An overview of Kauffman Firm Survey," *Ewing Marion Kauffman Foundation Research Paper*.

Robinson, K.C. (1999). "An examination of the influence of industry structure on eight alternative measures of new venture performance for high potential independent new ventures." *Journal of Business Venturing,* 14: 165-187.

Salomon, R., & Shaver, JM. (2005). "Export and domestic sales. Their interrelationships and determinants." *Strategic Management Journal.* 26:855-871.

Sapienza, H., Autio, E., George, G., & Zahra, S. (2006). "A Capabilities perspective on the effects of early internationalization on firm survival and growth." *Academy of Management Review,* 31(4):914-933.

Sapienza, H.J., De Clercq, D. Sandberg W.R. (2005). "Antecedents of international and domestic learning effort." *Journal of Business Venturing,* 20(4):437-457.

Saxenian, A. (2006). *The New Argonauts: Regional Advantage in a Global Economy.* Harvard University Press. Cambridge: MA.

Saxenian, A. (2002). "Silicon Valley's new immigrant high growth entrepreneurs." *Economic Development Quarterly,* 16(1):20-31.

Saxenian, A., & Hsu, J.-Y. (2001). "The Silicon Valley-Hsinchu connection: Technical communities and industrial upgrading." *Industrial and Corporate Change,* 4:893-920.

Saxenian, A. L. (1999). *Silicon Valley's New Immigrant Entrepreneurs.* San Francisco, CA: Public Policy Institute of California.

Schwens, C., Kabst, R. (2009a). "Early internationalization: A transaction cost economics and structural embeddedness perspective." *Journal of International Entrepreneurship,* 7(4), 323-340.

Schwens, C., Kabst, R. (2009b). "How early as opposed to late internationalizers learn: Experience of others and paradigms of interpretation." *International Business Review,* 18:509-522.

Shane, S. (2007). *The Illusions of Entrepreneurship: The Costly Myths that Entrepreneurs, Investors, and Policy Makers Live By.* Yale University Press.

Shane, S., & Cable, D. (2002). "Network ties, reputation, and the financing of new ventures." *Management Science,* 48(3):364-381.

Shane, S. (2000). "Prior knowledge and the discovery of entrepreneurial opportunities." *Organization Science,* 11(4):448-469.

Shane, S., & Venkataraman, S. (2000). "The promise of entrepreneurship as a field of research." *Academy of Management Review,* 25(1), 217-226

References

Shaver, J.M. (2005). "Testing for mediating variables in management research: Concerns, implications, and alternative strategies. *Journal of Management*, 31(3):330-353.

Shaver, J.M. (1998). "Accounting for endogeneity when assessing strategy performance: Does entry mode affect FDI survival?" *Management Science*, 44(4):571-585.

Shrader, R., Oviatt, B., & McDougall, P. (2000). "How ventures exploit tradeoffs among international risk factors: Lessons for accelerated internationalization of the 21st century." *Academy of Management Journal*, 43(6):1227-1247.

Simon, H.A. (1997). *An Empirically Based Microeconomics*. New York: Cambridge University Press.

Singh J.V., House, R. & Tucker, D.J. (1986). "Organizational change and organizational Mortality." *Admistrative Science Quarterly*, 31(4): 587-611.

Sirkin, H., Hemerling, J., & Bhattacharya, A. (2008). *Globality: Competing with Everyone from Everywhere for Everything*. New York, NY: Business Plus.

Stam, E. (2007). "Why butterflies don't leave: Locational behavior of entrepreneurial Firms." *Economic Geography*, 83(1):27-50.

Stinchcombe, A.L. (1965). "Social Structure and Organizations." In James March (Ed.), *Handbook of Organizations*. Chicago: Rand McNally.

Tabachnick, B. G. & Fidell, L. S. (2001). *Using Multivariate Statistics*. Fourth Edition. Allyn & Bacon Press. United States.

The Economist. (2009, March 12). *The United States of Entrepreneurs*. http://www.economist.com/node/13216037

Thomas, AS., & Mueller, A. (2000). "A case for comparative entrepreneurship: Assessing the relevance of culture." *Journal of International Business Studies*, 31(2):287-301.

Thompson, L. & Choi, S. (2006). *Creativity and Innovation in Organizational Teams*. LEA's Organization and Management Series.

Thornhill, S., & Amit, R. (2003). "Learning about failure: Bankruptcy, firm age and the resource based view," *Organization Science*, 14(5):497-509.

Tuppura, A., Saarenketo S., Puumalainen, K., Jsntunen, A., Kylaheiko K. (2008). "Linking knowledge, entry timing and internationalization strategy." *International Business Review*, 17(4), 473-487.

US Census Bureau. (2010). U.S. Department of Commerce, Washington, D.C.

US Department of State Publication (2008) http://www.america.gov/publications/ejournalusa/0508.html

Vinogradov, E. & Isaken, E. (2008). "Survival of new firms owned by natives and immigrants in Norway." *Journal of Developmental Entrepreneurship*, 13(1): 21-38.

Wadhwa, V., Rissing, B., AnnaLee, S., & Gereffi, G. (2007). Education, Entrepreneurship and Immigration: America's New Immigrant Entrepreneurs, Part I., Part II.

Westhead, P., Wright, M., & Ucbasaran, D. (2001). "The internationalization of new and small firms: A resource-based view." *Journal of Business Venturing*. 16:333-358.

Westhead, P. (1995). "Exporting and non-exporting small firms in Great Britain." *International Journal of Entrepreneurial Behavior & Research*. 1(2):6-36.

Wilson, K., & Portes, A. (1980). "Immigrant enclaves: An Analysis of the labor market experiences of Cubans in Miami." *The American Journal of Sociology*, 82(2): 113-152.

Wood, E., Khavul, S., Perez-Nordtvedt, L., Prakhya, S., Velarde, R., & Zheng, C. (2011). "Strategic commitment and timing of internationalization: Evidence from China, India, Mexico and South Africa." *Journal of Small Business Management*, in press.

Wright, R.E. (1995). "Logistic regression". In L.G. Grimm & P.R. Yarnold, eds., *Reading and Understanding Multivariate Statistics*. Washington, DC: American Psychological Association.

Yeoh, P. (2004). "International learning: antecedents and performance implications among newly internationalizing companies in an exporting context". *International Marketing Review*, 21(4/5): 511-535.

Yin, R.K. (2002). *Case Study Research: Design and Methods*. Sage Publications. 3rd Ed.

Yuki, M. (2003). "Intergroup comparison versus intragroup relationships: A cross-cultural examination of social identity theory in North American and East Asian cultural contexts." *Social Psychology Quarterly*, 66: 66-183.

Zacharakis, A. (1997). Entrepreneurial entry into foreign markets: A transaction cost perspective, *Entrepreneurship Theory and Practice*, 21: 23-39.

References

Zahra, S.A, (2005). "A Theory of International New Ventures: A decade of Research," *Journal of International Business Studies*, 36: 20-28.

Zahra, S., & George, G. (2002). "International entrepreneurship: the current status of the field and future research agenda." In M. Hitt, D. Ireland, M. Camp, & D. Sexton, *Strategic Entrepreneurship: Creating a New Mindset* (pp. 255-288). Oxford: Blackwell Publishing.

Zahra, S., Ireland, R., & Hitt, M. (2000). "International expansion by new venture firms: International diversity, mode of market entry, technological learning and performance." *Academy of Management Journal*, 43:925-950.

Zaheer, S. (2002). "The Liability of foreignness, Redux: A Commentary," *Journal of International Management*, 8(3): 351-358.

Zaheer, S., Lamin, A., & Subramani, M. (2009). "Cluster capabilities or ethnic ties? Location choice by foreign and domestic entrants in the services offshoring industry in India." *Journal of International Business Studies*, 40:944-968.

Zaheer, S., & Zaheer, A. (2006). "Trust across borders." *Journal of International Business Studies*, 37(1): 21-29.

Zaheer, S., Mosakowski, E. (1997). "The dynamics of the liabilities of foreignness." *Strategic Management Journal*, 18(6): 439-464.

Zaheer, S. (1995). "Overcoming the liabilities of foreignness." *Academy of Management Journal*, 38(2):341-363.

Zander, I. (2004). "The micro foundations of cluster stickiness – walking in the shoes of the entrepreneur." *Journal of International Management*, 10:151-175.

Zhou, L., Barnes, B., Lu, Y. (2010). "Entrepreneurial proclivity, capability upgrading and performance advantage of newness among international new ventures." *Journal of International Business Studies*, 41(5): 882-905.

Zhou, L., Wu, W., Luo, X. (2007). "Internationalization and the performance of born-global SMEs: the mediating role of social networks." *Journal of International Business Studies*, 38: 673-690.

Index

Behavioral theory of the firm, 30-31
Cognitive barriers, 3, 32, 107
Cost of doing business abroad, 34-35, 37
Early internationalziation, 4, 12, 40
   antecedents, 14-17
   benefits, 12-13
   costs, 13-14
   outcomes, 17-18
Endogeneity, 59, 63
Entrepreneurs
   education, 111
   need for achievement, 86, 88-89, 98
   need for autonomy, 94-95, 98
   overconfidence, 113-114, 116
   previous experience, 111
   pressure for success, 99-100, 113-114, 116
Experiential knowledge, 3, 10, 26
Global mindset, 32, 104
High technology startups, 3, 41-42
Immigrant
   entrepreneurship, 1, 119-120
   low-tech, 23
   high-tech, 24-25
   status, 4, 40

Insider entrepreneurs, 25-27
International entrepreneurship, 12, 118-119
International new ventures, 1, 7-9
Interviews, 83
   process, 84-86
   findings 86-102
Learning advanatges of newness, 36
Liabilities of foreigness, 34-35, 37, 119
Liabilities of newness, 9, 13, 110, 119
Kaufman firm survey, 4, 42-44
McCraken, 84-86
McDougall, 7, 10, 12, 17, 124
New Venture
   financing, 91-93, 100-101
   growth, 4, 18, 36-40, 111-112
   resources, 97, 109-110
   scalability, 90, 98-99
   survival, 4, 17, 34-36, 37-39, 40, 110-111
Outsider entrepreneurs, 2, 25-27
Outsidership, 27
Outsourcing, 97
Relational barriers, 3, 34, 107
Robustness of results, 78-8

Routines, 31, 36, 38-39
Research questions, 4
Saxenian, 3, 24
Self-employement, 21-22
Simon, 30
Social embededdness, 3, 26
Strategic management, 120-121
Study findings, 53-81
Study limitations, 124–125
Study purpose, 1-2
Study significance, 2-3, 5
Variables
  control, 49-52
  definitions, 47-48
  dependent, 45-46
  independent, 46
United States, 3, 7, 41, 92, 107, 123-124

WITHDRAWN